¡Sí Se Puede!

Learning from a High School That Beats the Odds

¡Sí Se Puede!

Learning from a High School That Beats the Odds

Úrsula Casanova

Foreword by Gloria Ladson-Billings

Teachers College, Columbia University
New York and London

Published by Teachers College Press, 1234 Amsterdam Avenue, New York, NY
10027

Library of Congress Cataloging-in-Publication Data

Casanova, Úrsula.
¡Sí se puede! : learning from a high school that beats the odds / Úrsula Casanova ;
foreword by Gloria Ladson-Billings.
    p. cm.
    Includes bibliographical references and index.
    ISBN 978-0-8077-5102-2 (pbk. : alk. paper)
    1. Cibola High School (Yuma, Ariz.)—Case studies. 2. Hispanic Americans—
Education (Secondary)—Arizona—Yuma—Case studies. 3. School improvement
programs—Arizona—Yuma—Case studies. I. Title.
    LD7501.Y86C37 2010
    373.79.1'71—dc22   2010011946

ISBN 978-0-8077-5102-2 (paper)

Printed on acid-free paper

Manufactured in the United States of America

17 16 15 14 13 12 11 10   8 7 6 5 4 3 2 1

Contents

7. Conclusion

Foreword

I began researching successful teachers of African American students some 20 years ago because almost all of the literature that focused on African American students was cast in deficit language. An electronic search of the literature on African American education very quickly defaulted to "see, 'culturally deprived'" or "see, 'culturally disadvantaged.'" The implication was that there was no excellence or exemplary practice occurring in schools serving African American students. Even though Sara Lawrence-Lightfoot had written about "Good High Schools" in 1985, her narratives were received as if race or culture were ancillary to the goodness described.

In ¡Sí Se Puede! Úrsula Casanova explores how Cibola High School, located in the southwestern United States, succeeds in effectively educating Latino(a) students. The story of Cibola's excellence is not shocking to me. I have spent the last 22 years seeking out pockets of excellence in places where others suggest that no such excellence exists. What Casanova does in this book is add to the "existence proofs" that I have insisted were available all along. In Cibola High School, Casanova finds a sustained effort at excellence that in some ways mirrors the early work of Ron Edmonds and others who insisted that a rather limited set of correlates—a clear and focused mission, instructional leadership, regular monitoring of student achievement, opportunity to learn and time on task, a safe and orderly environment, and good home–school relations—is the key to success for all students.

Cibola High School, as Casanova describes it, addresses each of these correlates and helps the reader understand what they look like in action. With clear and lively writing, the reader comes to know Cibola High School, its leaders, and the stability that characterized school life on the campus. Seemingly simple strategies such as closing the campus, focusing on a college preparatory curriculum, and carefully staffing the school created an atmosphere of high expectation and high aspirations.

This is the kind of book pre-service teachers, educational foundations students, and in-service teachers working in a changing demographic environment need to read. They need to re-orient their perspectives about the students they are teaching and where they need to help those students get to. This is the kind of book that can become canonical for teachers.

I am especially glad that this book deals with a high school because much of the literature on successful practice (my own work included) focuses on elementary classrooms. In elementary schools, the fact that the students are in self-contained classrooms with one teacher helps researchers eliminate a variety of variables. High schools, on the other hand, are extremely complex ecologies. The students rotate between four to seven teachers in a typical day. They arrive at high school with extensive educational resumes, including their elementary and middle school experiences, their involvement with tutors and afterschool programs, their loose peer-group affiliations and participation in tightly scheduled youth activities. Isolating "effective practice" in the midst of these competing variables is a formidable task for researchers.

Casanova was smart enough to keep an ear to the ground and allow what community members said about the school to guide her curiosity. Her fundamental questions became, "Is this school as good as they say it is? What is the secret to its goodness?" She could rather easily answer the first question. The data, as researchers like to say, speak for themselves. Students were graduating from Cibola *and* they were going on to postsecondary education. The second question reflects the research journey. What will she find beneath the numbers? How will her observations and interviews elaborate the numbers? Who are the people (administrators, faculty, students, parents, and community members) who make those numbers come alive?

In this volume, Casanova helps us see both the simple and complex factors involved in creating excellent schools for students who traditionally fail at schooling. On the simple side, we see obvious things like visionary leadership, high expectations, and faculty and staff stability. These features of successful schools are supported by literature that goes back decades. However, Casanova also exposes the more complex work of maintaining these criteria over time and between and within the community, parents, students, teachers, and administrators. This work relies on a delicate balance and a deep sense of community and culture to build what scholars who examine school reform call "relational trust" (Bryk & Schneider, 2003).

¡*Si Se Puede!* is more than a catchy slogan or rallying cry; it is a worldview and a philosophy for ensuring that Latino(a) students experience the educational excellence they, their parents, and their community expect and desire. This is the kind of story that our teachers, both pre-service and in-service, need to know in order to expand their own perspectives about the possibility of educating all students. This is the contribution to the literature on excellence we have been waiting for.

—*Gloria Ladson-Billings,*
University of Wisconsin–Madison

REFERENCES

Bryk, A., & Schneider, B. (2003, March). Trust in schools: A core resource for school reform. *Educational Leadership, 60*(6), 40–44.

Lawrence-Lightfoot, S. (1985). *The good high school: Portraits of character and culture.* New York: Basic Books.

Acknowledgments

One of the interesting facts about this book is that it is the result of an effort to learn more about dropouts, particularly Latino(a) dropouts, in Arizona. That was the task I was assigned by Gene García, who was at that time the newly appointed Dean of Education at Arizona State University. It was through my research for my job that I became aware of O. Ricardo Pimentel, editor of the opinion page for the *Arizona Republic,* who discovered and wrote about Cibola High School. His description of a high school where Latino(a) students were not only graduating but continuing on to college was hard to believe at a time when Arizona's graduation rate hovered around 60% for the state (the rate was much lower for Latino(a) students). My first thanks go to Pimentel for writing that enticing essay and to Eugene García, now vice president for university/school relationships, for encouraging my interest and supporting my research so that we could bring the Cibola story to a wider audience.

My involvement began with a search for the truth. Was Cibola really succeeding as Pimentel said, or was it all smoke and mirrors? I was able to uncover the answer to this question through the kindness of so many of the people who contributed to Cibola's creation and its continued development. Among them, a few require special mention. Jon Walk, the first principal and spiritual mentor of Cibola High School, was willing to share the story of Cibola's creation with me. The principals who followed him—Gary Wiersema, now in Indiana, and Johnny Rico, now retired from the Yuma Union High School District (YUHSD)—were both willing to share their memories of Cibola through writing and conversation.

I must thank the many teachers and counselors, from the veterans who were there when the school opened to the brand-new arrivals who had themselves graduated from Cibola, for giving me their valuable time so I could understand how it felt to be a teacher at this school. For the most part, they must remain anonymous. I am also grateful to the similarly anonymous students who were kind enough to put up with my questions and thus allow me to see what it was like to be a student at Cibola High School.

This book could not have been written without the support of three key administrators who for the last 5 years have been willing to answer my incessant questions: YUHSD superintendent Toni Badone, Cibola's principal Tony Steen, and Cibola's head of guidance Becky García. They have been beyond patient with me and have not only submitted to long interviews, but also have searched for answers to questions I brought up that they had not yet considered.

I am indebted, as well, to my academic colleagues—among them Jeannie Oakes, Sonia Nieto, Linda Darling-Hammond, and Gustavo Fischman—who, upon hearing my stories about Cibola, encouraged me to write this book and bring the story to the public. Most persistent among them was my closest friend, my colleague and husband David Berliner, who insisted that the book should be written and was there to reassure me as I took the first steps toward that goal. Equally supportive were our five children, their partners, and our grandchildren, whose love and support have made the task easier.

I also want to express my deep appreciation to my editor, Jean Ward, for her encouragement, guidance, and especially for her patience as the Cibola story traveled with me across the months and miles.

Finally, I hope that those who have been a part of Cibola's birth, growth, and continued success will find that this book represents their school well and will also accept my apologies for any misquotes or misrepresentations that may have escaped me.

Introduction:
The Cibola Story

It is a late afternoon in December. The school has emptied out. Two counselors are still in the office after a busy day going over students' schedules. One of the counselors sits at her desk in her office; the other one is standing by the office door. I'm across the room from them. They are complaining gently about the many last-minute changes being requested by the students. I ask, "Why do you allow them? Hasn't the deadline (clearly posted on the door) passed?" Both counselors respond simultaneously: "It's their life!" That is, the choices the students make will affect them for life, thus they should have the freedom to make as many changes as necessary.

Selecting electives is a very important process at Cibola High School, where schedules are not built by computers. Two people—the assistant principal of academics and the head of guidance and counseling—construct each semester's program by hand. Although there is little latitude regarding the required courses, elective choices are wide open for students. So students meet with their assigned counselors every semester to check their progress on required credits and make their choice of electives. But these are teenagers, and they have trouble making up their minds, so they often return to ask for changes. That is why the deadline, while desirable, may not work for all students. The question remains: Why are the counselors so accepting of their students' demands, which are often hugely inconvenient for them?

It goes back to 1988, or perhaps 1987, when Jon Walk, the school's first principal, was given a year to plan for and hire the staff for the new high school being built in Yuma, Arizona. That first principal had a very clear idea of what that new high school should be. He saw opening that new school as an opportunity, "a chance to start something brand new, from scratch. . . . It's a great gift." So he set out to develop, with his chosen assistants and department heads, a philosophy for a school where "we would make a difference. . . . [W]e would help kids be successful. . . . [W]e believed it, stated it, put it in writing . . . posted our mission statement all over the school, and it's still there."

Walk's determination was born out of "seeing so much frustration in schools, so much student frustration about . . . not achieving. Seeing a lot of faculty frustration where you could see the faculty [was] real unhappy . . . because they didn't believe they could make a difference. They had lost hope in themselves and in the kids." His frustration with the way things were gave him the hope and determination to plan for a *really* new high school where all students would be expected to succeed.

But it takes more than hope and determination to create a new school and to ensure student success. Walk was also blessed with an unerring instinct for selecting the right people to accompany him on his journey toward excellence. Among them was Jim Sullivan, who became head of guidance and whose involvement in the school would be an essential component in Cibola's success.

Sullivan, or "Sully" as everyone still calls him, understood that students' expectations were framed within the limits of the possibilities they saw for themselves. He believed that his role as a counselor was to open up windows into alternative futures and then provide students with the support to realize them. Thus, the office of guidance and counseling became "the heart of the school." At Cibola, a high school diploma would no longer be the end goal. That diploma was only a stepping-stone to a more distant but wholly achievable future. The guidance counselors were responsible for applying their collective energy to ensuring the realization of their students' loftier aspirations. The footprints of these two men, and of the leadership staff they selected, are still visible more than 20 years later, in the daily operation of the school. The counselors cited above, who placed their students' needs above their clerical requirements, exemplify the school's original purpose.

I was introduced to Cibola High School by an article in the local newspaper which described the success of a high school close to the Arizona border that served primarily Latino(a) students. The author, Pimentel, noted the school's success not only in retaining students through graduation but also in sending most of them on for further education. This was unheard of in Arizona, where the Latino(a) high school graduation rate hovers around 60%. It was also of great interest to me, as I was just beginning a research project on Arizona dropouts with a particular emphasis on Latinos(as).

So I went to Yuma, and during my first visit to Cibola High School, I spoke to Anthony (Tony) Steen, the principal of the school, as well as to several guidance counselors. I was impressed by their willingness to speak to me openly, to answer my questions, and to display documents illustrating their statements. Everything I heard and saw appeared to confirm Pimentel's assertions.[1] I was hooked. Cibola appeared to be a positive outlier against the dismal statistics of school completion in Arizona. I had to learn more about what was happening at this school to account for that distinction while also avoiding being misguided by first impressions.

The story that follows is based on 4 years of data derived from observations, interviews, and archival documents. Throughout those years, I learned enough to convince me that what this school has accomplished through its more than 20-year history is a powerful anomaly. I believe that at a time when the nation seems to be engaged in a continuous losing battle for high school reform, we must look to Cibola High School as existence proof of what is possible.

AN OUTLINE OF THE BOOK

In Chapter 1, I address Cibola's history and the imprint of that history on Cibola today. Chapter 2 follows with an analysis of what I have identified as the key elements of Cibola's success, beginning with the founding concept of the school: high expectations. The influence and lasting power of leadership is addressed in Chapter 3, followed by a look at Cibola's counseling and guidance program and its essential role in achieving the founders' dreams in Chapter 4. The importance of English instruction for English learners, a latecomer to Cibola's continuous effort to fulfill its promise, is discussed in Chapter 5, followed by an analysis of other curriculum components that have emerged through the years in response to specific needs in Chapter 6. In the final chapter, Chapter 7, I offer my conclusions.

Chapter One

Cibola's History

Cibola High School's history is worthy of special attention because it challenges the assumptions commonly held about minority populations in the United States, specifically about Black and Latino(a) schoolchildren. With the exception of students of Asian background, minority students are expected to occupy the bottom rung of the educational ladder at most high schools in the United States. That is unfortunate but not surprising; because they are also more likely to be poor and to have less-schooled parents (see Table 1.1), such students are almost always found well below the median when compared to White middle-class and Asian students in the same schools.

Sadly, this permanent "achievement gap" has become a demographic destiny that is accepted by the students, their teachers, and sometimes even their parents as a given condition of their heritage and low socio-economic position. And yet data from the National Center for Education Statistics (NCES)[1] tell us that there is no longer a statistical difference in the expectations for higher education across U.S. income groups (see Chapter 2, Table 2.3).

Table 1.1. Percent of Parents' Highest Level of Education and Racial/Ethnic Group Among High School Sophomores

Parents' Education Level	African American	Asian/Pacific Islander	Hispanic/ Latino(a)	White	American Indian/ Alaska Native	Multiracial
Less than high school	4.8	10.2	23.4	2.2	7.5	4.2
High school only	22	14.5	23.0	20.3	23.1	18.1
Some college	8	23.3	32.4	34.6	40.4	40.5
4 yr. degree	41.5	28.7	13.8	24.1	16.8	21.7
Graduate or professional degree	19.2	23.3	7.4	18.8	12.3	15.6

I have come to understand that the faculty and staff at Cibola High School do not accept a demographic destiny for their charges. Their eyes are firmly fixed on the potential that may be hidden or overlooked but that nonetheless is present in every one of their students. And they have been doing that for over 20 years! Cibola's records (see Table 1.2) consistently show that they graduate over 95% of their seniors and that almost every one of those graduating students continues on to post-secondary education. The vast majority of their students go on to 2- or 4-year colleges, while about 10% will choose trade schools or join the military.

Cibola is clearly an exception. Its history demonstrates how the be-lief system that guides the actions of many education professionals serv-ing minority students can shape the decisions they make about them. Cibola also hints at the reasons why many school reform efforts fail to make or sustain the expected gains in the graduation and postsecondary placements of the students they serve. In other school reform efforts, the teachers do not really believe their students can reach those goals, and their own low expectations are internalized by their students. That is why reforms may appear on the surface, but, like the waves in the ocean, nothing changes in the depths.

Table 1.2. Cibola High School—Annual Profiles for Alternate Classes, 1996–2008.

Category	1996	1998	2000	2002	2004	2006	2008
Enrollment	2,410	2,353	2,418	2,650	2,616	2,384	2,377
Ethnicity	65%H 30%A 5% other	69%H 26%A 5% other	72%H 24%A 4% other	73%H 23%A 4% other	74%H 22%A 4% other	74%H 22%A 4% other	75%H 20%A 5% other
Migrants	46%	34%	29%	28%	28%	19%	14%
AP Courses	3	3	3	4	5	9	6
AP Enrollment	70 (1.6%)	82 (3.4%)	93 (4%)	184 (7%)	114 (4%)	429 (18%)	566 (24%)
Honors Courses	14	15	15	15	13	10	11 (Accel classes)
Honors Enrollment	600 (25%)	1,242 (53%)	1,321 (55%)	1,284 (48%)	970 (37%)	823 (35%)	860 (36%)
Dual credit	—	—	234 (10%)	224 (8%)	56 (2%)	69 (3%)	97 (4%)
SAT	V: 532 M: 540	V: 524 M: 528	V: 526 M: 528	V: 526 M: 528	V: 535 M: 536	V: 512 M: 535	V: 511 M: 524
ACT (Comp.)	22.4	21.9	20.9	20.9	21.5	20.5	23.1
4-year Post-HS	24%	24%	24%	33%	42%	39%	39%
2-year Post-HS	65%	65%	65%	56%	47%	49%	49%
Trade/Military/ Work	5% trade 6% mil/wk	5% trade 6% mil/wk	5% trade 6% mil/wk	5% trade 6% mil/wk	5% trade 6% mil/wk	5% trade 7% mil/wk	6% trade 6% mil/wk

Cibola High School's early history and subsequent development can help us understand the reasons for its success. It is a story that can best be told through the voices of the people who created or witnessed it. Jon Walk was the leader of that enterprise, but there were many others, some of whom remain at Cibola, some who have moved on to the district offices, and some who have retired. Through the years I have had the opportunity to interview many of them and found so much unanimity across their statements that, in my mind, they have become a multivocal chorus. Here is how they recall Cibola's beginnings.

AT THE BEGINNING

Cibola's story began when John Walk was selected to lead the new school in 1986, almost 2 years before its opening. He recalls:

> That gave me the time to develop the philosophy for the school with a group of teachers from Yuma. . . . Almost half of the staff came from the two existing Yuma schools. . . . [The district] gave me the opportunity to gather and recruit from all over the country . . . and I was able to hire top quality, really good, progressive, energetic young people. . . . They had a real strong sense of efficacy, and they were eager to go out there and make a difference for kids. . . . The people who came from the existing Yuma high schools were good people that were looking for change, . . . for community, . . . for a site that would be different, that would be more progressive, that would be trying a new way of doing things. We had a lot of people who believed that schools are for kids and that we can make a difference in the life of kids, both academically and socially. The school was built on the philosophy that we would make a difference, that we would help kids be successful.

Gary Wiersema, one of the original vice principals, echoes Walk's words:

> Jon had great vision. . . . [B]asically teachers could apply to come to the new school, Jon would interview them, and . . . we got to choose the best teachers. If there wasn't someone [in Yuma] to fill the position, we got to go looking for the best teachers in other states like Montana, Iowa, and Indiana, to name a few. Department chairs were the first ones we went after, some we recruited, others just wanted to come because they were ready for something

new. The basic foundation we wanted was high high-energy, cre-
ative teaching, you have to like kids and will do whatever it takes
for them to be successful. In return, as administrators, we would do
everything we could to create the best possible learning environment and to do whatever it takes for the teachers to be successful
in their jobs of educating kids.

The person chosen by Walk to head Cibola's social studies department, Johnny Rico, elaborates on Walk's vision:

> [T]he vision was . . . that the school was student-centered and all
> decisions that would be made . . . would be in the best interest of
> the kids. We also felt that we had to have not only teachers that
> had a strong academic background but . . . they had to have that
> passion . . . the passion that we all had toward our field and, more
> important than that, toward the education of our students. And so,
> that was something we instilled in our people. And . . . that focus
> came from all departments in the selection of their teachers.

Jon Walk notes that wanting to make a difference in kids' lives is every school's and district's philosophy, but he adds:

> I think that we believed it, stated it, put it in writing, posted our
> mission statement on every wall in the school and it's still there.
> The mission statement . . . is still there. . . . We were truly commit-
> ted to it. It drove our decisions; it drove the way we behaved.

Walk was able to hire both assistant principals and his department
chairpersons a year before Cibola opened. That allowed them time to
leave Yuma for a weekend to develop their mission statement.

STATING CIBOLA'S MISSION

Johnny Rico recalled how Cibola's mission statement was created:

> The mission was developed by the original administrative team at
> [Cibola], which included the department chairs and our mainte-
> nance supervisor. [We] all went to a retreat in the Phoenix area and
> we spent about 2½ days discussing roles [and] expectations. But
> the main objective of that particular retreat was to come up with a
> mission statement. [T]here were so many different ideas that were

being offered, and I thought at that time . . . that Mr. Walk did a great job of keeping us all focused and on-course of where, in his mind, he felt we should be. And we came up with the mission: "Cibola is committed to success and to challenging students and staff to reach their highest potential." And we were very proud of that one.

The mission created by the leadership team was well received by the rest of the faculty. "[W]hen they came back . . . it was a success," recalls Toni Badone, one of the original English teachers.

Challenging students and staff to achieve their highest potential, it was so simple. . . . We were all about "let's do it right plus make sure our kids are successful." . . . The good thing about that mission was that we could really use it as a measuring stick for decisions: Is this going to help us with this mission? If not, is it that important? Unless the law says we have to do it, let's not worry about it. Not quite that simple but, does it contribute? If not . . . let's put it over here (as she moves one hand to her side). Let's put our focus on this (signaling the center with her hand).

Badone also remembers what drew her to move:

I wanted an opportunity to teach in a school where there was this very specific mission, the emphasis being on the need to eliminate that ceiling, the glass ceiling that we have as teachers, the kids have, the parents have, in this community about what they can do. Just because they're in Yuma, Arizona, that doesn't mean they can't go to Stanford or Harvard. . . . [Also,] it was a fun place to work. People had fun with each other, but we worked so hard . . . 14 to 16 hours a day . . . because we just knew we could do a better job. . . . It was just, "let's take the ceiling off it . . . see how far we can go . . . increase expectations."

Unfortunately, the enthusiasm that Cibola's eager faculty brought to the plans for the new school was not echoed by their soon-to to-be students. As Jon Walk recalls:

Ironically, the very first thing that I faced before we opened was sort of an outcry from the parents of a lot of kids who were supposed to go to Cibola and said "I don't want to go . . . we don't want to go. . . ." It was really hurtful to hear that. . . . And the main reason they didn't want to go was that we opened with (only) ninth and tenth graders. So they said, "We don't want to go to a school where there are no seniors and no juniors and there's no varsity sports program. . . . [A]nd we don't want to be the guinea pigs that have to get everything going."

The angry reaction from their future students was a big disappointment to a faculty so strongly motivated by their desire to be the best teachers. So, Cibola's leadership team began holding meetings in the various schools where the students would be coming from to introduce the staff, department chairs, coaches, and band director to everyone around town. And soon, says Jon, "They started to say, 'Hey, you know what, this place is going to be all right. These people have a lot on the ball. These people are excited, they're energetic,' that was how we drew the community in."

BEYOND HIGH SCHOOL GRADUATION

Any conversation about Cibola's success quickly turns to the guidance office and its contribution to the fulfillment of the school's mission. Counseling and guidance were a major concern and became a major contributor to the school's success. Walk hired Jim (Sully) Sullivan, a well-respected counselor and colleague from his former school. Sully had very clear ideas about what needed to be done in that area:

> As the head of guidance, I instituted the 4-year plan. I thought that every kid should go beyond high school and that the best way to ensure that was by having everyone follow a 4-year plan. It could be a 4- or 2-year college, or a technical school, but everyone should go beyond high school. And every teacher we hired had to think that way as well.

This was at a time when only 51% of U.S. Hispanics were completing a high school degree and a mere 10% had completed a BA or higher. Jim Sullivan, the head of Cibola's original office of guidance, personified high expectations.

The quotes above well illustrate how determined Cibola's leadership was to ensure the success of every one of their students. And, by design, success at Cibola was not going to be defined by their students' high school diplomas but by their continuation of education beyond high school. At the new school in town the goalposts were shifted for the

1988 entering class and all those that would follow. Cibola's graduates would be expected, and guided, to continue their education after high school, whether at colleges, universities , trade schools, or the military.

But doing the implementation of this plan was not always easy. There were many long hours and many frustrations as the school took shape. In addition, there was some tension in the district. Thirty years had passed since the opening of Kofa, the second high school in the city. Thus, Cibola was the first new school in a long time, and the lofty ideals proclaimed by the newcomer presented a challenge that was not totally welcomed by their peers. Badone says,

> We were all so excited . . . running around this great new school. [T]he people who didn't choose to come to Cibola were usually a little put off by the overabundance of enthusiasm, and they would make these comments [like]. . . "Well, how is it down at Paradise Valley?" Or they would say, "Well, how is it down at Little Harvard?" We were going to send every kid to college and they teased us. Finally, about 3 summers after we'd opened, we figured out a T-shirt [design], and we had a student, one of my English (class) students, design it. I bought a Harvard T-shirt, and we replaced the ivy with palm trees and in that little shield instead of "veritas" it said "Cibolas." And then we put "Little Harvard on the Colorado." . . . You know, you had to have fun with it. (See Figure 1.1.)

Jon Walk is the person mainly credited for Cibola's success by all those who were there at the beginning. However, credit must also be given to then-Superintendant Browne. He not only made a wise choice by selecting Jon, and doing so a full year and a half before the school was to open, but he also allowed Jon to select his leadership team early and to take them on a retreat. That extra time allowed the top administrators not only to create Cibola's mission statement but also to develop working relationships with one another and discuss at some leisure the kind of school they wanted Cibola to be and how they wanted to get there. All of that probably contributed to the weight and consistency of the message received by the rest of the faculty when the school opened.

Perry Hill, who arrived in Yuma to become the high school district's new assistant superintendent the same year Cibola opened, recalls his first get-acquainted visit to the three district high schools:

> I came in about a week before the school openings . . . and visited all the campuses, and right away I knew Cibola was different. It had high energy. The other thing was that Jon had a vision of

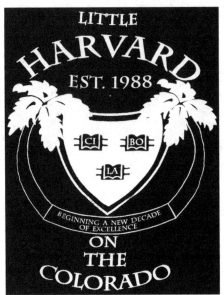

Figure1.1. Cibola High School T-Shirt Design.

the future and he knew that he had to build history and set the foundation. . . . And, because he got to pick his people, because he had that vision, because he got people that were interested in the kids, especially the Latino(a) population, because of the mission that they set, the whole school was just different. . . . When you give that vision to kids, you have better attendance, you have fewer discipline problems, and you have kids focusing on academics. And the first day those kids walked into that school the message that they got was, "you don't have a choice about achieving; you will achieve."

As Hill notes, Walk's main contribution was having a well-developed vision of what the new school could be—a vision that transcended his experience, as well as the experiences of those he chose to accompany him on that journey. Their words suggest their frustration with their previously self-imposed "glass ceiling" that kept them and their students from entertaining higher aspirations. The vision was also personally seductive. It represented the dreams many teachers have as they begin their careers: to change the world, to empower the unempowered, to embrace a common goal with peers, and to work together to achieve it. And so they followed him, fully trusting in their leader as well as in their collective power to make a significant difference in the lives of their students.

Walk made the most of the time he was given to think and to plan to make his vision a reality. He traveled around the country, attended lectures, and read current educational research that, at the time, included Edmond's and Lezzote's research on the correlates of effective schools (see www.effectiveschools.com for more on their work), which found "high expectations" and the role of the principal were considered essential.

HIRING THE BEST TEACHERS

Once the transfers from the other Yuma high schools were selected, Walk and occasionally his assistants went out and hired teachers from distant states to complete Cibola's faculty. Besides being well trained, those selected also had to buy into the school's vision. They had to believe that all kids could learn and succeed not only in high school but beyond. They had to have high expectations for every single one of the school's students.

The expectations of the Cibola staff were especially daring when you consider that, as Perry Hill notes, they were going to be facing a difficult population. The community of Sommerton was angry because they had wanted the new high school to be built in their neighborhood. Hill remembers:

> There was extreme tension, potential tension, between the kids [from] there and Sommerton being bused in. Even parents were heard to say: "[W]e don't want 'those' kids here . . . let them go someplace else."

When it was finally time for the school to open, all was not well. The district delayed the opening of school that year until the day after Labor Day to ensure that the new school would be ready, but as Walk remembers, there was still work to do: "The day before we opened we were still down there sweeping parking lots, throwing boxes away, you name it. . . . [W]e were working there until midnight that Sunday night, and Monday was Labor Day. . . . [I]t was like a real family—let's roll up our sleeves, get down to work, and make this a good deal." Walk continues:

> We wanted the place to appear bright, cheery, clean, organized, and, most important—and this is what we built the school on—we wanted the staff to connect immediately with the kids. We wanted the kids to walk out of here feeling, "you know, these people seem to care about us. . . . [T]hey're not here just to tell us where

we're supposed to be, they want to make a difference in my life
and they're going to push me to try to make a difference. . . ." We
wanted everybody to leave with that impression from day one.

The day finally came for Cibola High School to open its doors. Everyone was putting on the last touches when the buses arrived, a full 40
minutes before they were expected! Gary Wiersema, assistant principal
of discipline, remembers: "It was a real emergency. Cibola's school yard
was going to be the setting for the very first face-to-face meeting of rival
gangs from Sommerton and the West Side. And the school would not
open for 40 minutes." Fortunately, the adults prevailed, and when the
bell rang everyone moved into their classes peacefully.

However, gangs continued to be a problem during the first year, says
Wiersema. Before Cibola, the enmity didn't arise in school—it was out
there in Yuma—and there were few problems as long as the gangs were
separated. Cibola forced the gangs together and, thus, conflicts arose,
particularly during that first year.

As the assistant principal of discipline, Gary Wiersema bore the
brunt of that tension. "We had lots of suspensions at the start," he says.
They managed the problem by getting to know the kids, developing
trust in one another, and demonstrating the staff's concern for their students. They formed personal relationships with the students by enlisting
the family's support and communicating their interest in the students'
success. Wiersema says that, at the beginning, when he or Walk visited
students' homes, parents would feel intimidated and would have to
be reassured that the school had their child's best interest at heart. But,
he adds, "When you take time to meet someone at their house, you're
showing respect and concern for their child."

Former superintendent Hill remembers how the staff brought the
kids in and started to work on them right away: "There were programs
to integrate not segregate. . . . [T]hey integrated sports, the arts, music.
. . . [Y]ou could never go to CHS without adults being in the hallways.
And they had programs for kids where they would mix and share. . . .
[W]hat [the school] did is they taught [the kids] to work together."

Hill says there certainly was tension, but it was not the main issue
thanks to the efforts of the staff: "I think the main difference was that at
Cibola the kids knew that they were cared about, even in high school.
The staff, under Jon's leadership, was able to convince them that they
could achieve and [that they] were important . . . that education was important. And I think the kids responded to that."

Jon Walk remained Cibola's principal for the next 4 years, after which he became assistant superintendent at the district office and Gary Wiersema became Cibola's principal.

The history of Cibola High School, as described its founders, sets the stage for the chapters that follow. An idealistic, caring leader; a succinct, clearly stated mission; a faculty chosen as much for their values as for their educational training; and a beautiful, brand-new building all provided the new school with fertile soil for future success, but these things did not assure that success. The high expectations everyone brought to the task was an important component, but how could those expectations be translated into student success? And how long could it last?

The daily routines, the decisions made, and the actions taken are the tools through which an organization operates. They form the context within which a mission may be accomplished. And much of that was carefully set down at the very beginning. But how has it been possible to sustain that original mission through more than 20 years?

For the last 4 years, I have been trying to identify the components that have been essential to Cibola's consistent success, not just in graduating the vast majority of students, but also in sending most of them on for further education. I have identified five components of Cibola's success: high expectations, leadership, counseling and guidance, the instruction of English learners, and the continuous search for improvement that has led to alternative roads to success. All of these are highly interrelated. It is the combination of all of them that has allowed Cibola to achieve well beyond its demographic destiny. Some of the components were not there at the beginning. Indeed, one of the characteristics that has impressed me about Cibola has been the way in which the school has repeatedly responded to perceived problems by applying solutions derived from practice or research, or both, and how the proposed solutions are always pilot-tested before full implementation. Each of the five components will be examined in the chapters that follow, beginning with high expectations.

Chapter Two

High Expectations

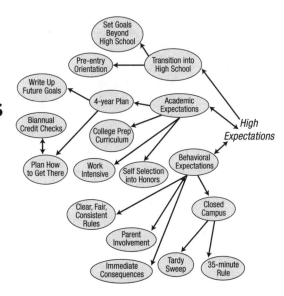

Before we continue Cibola's story, let's take a look at the educational environment around the time Cibola was conceived and established. What were eighth graders like at that time? What about Hispanic students? What were their hopes and expectations in 1988, the year Cibola opened?

THE EDUCATIONAL CONDITION OF THE AGE COHORT

By a happy coincidence, Cibola opened the same year that the National Center for Education Statistics (NCES) published a comprehensive national study of eighth graders in the United States. The study, called the National Education Longitudinal Survey of 1988 (NELS:88), included five major racial/ethnic groups: American Indian, Asian, Black, Hispanic, and White. The report gathered data about the social conditions of eighth graders in the United States, as well as their school achievement and aspirations for the future. The results revealed the high aspirations held by those soon-to-be high school students. Over two-thirds of the students in each of the racial/ethnic groups were expecting to go to college. Almost 72% of Latinos(as), the group that made up the highest proportion of Cibola's entering students, expressed their intentions to attend college. The authors of NELS:88 concluded that:

> Most students *do* plan to succeed in school. But often, students are simply unaware of the consequences of their program selections and how such selections

may place them on certain tracks both in school and in life. Perhaps one way to help students succeed in high school would be to distribute in the middle grades more information on different high school programs and how they relate to various postsecondary academic and vocational program requirements. Encouraging greater parental involvement in high school planning might promote more realistic program plans and expectations.[1] (emphasis in original)

That is, of course, what the Cibola staff did. They went out to the middle schools to announce to entering students and their parents the new school's high expectations for the incoming class. They did not limit themselves to the importance of staying in school to get a high school diploma; instead, they urged their students to begin thinking about their postsecondary choices. Although such talk was probably unusual in most Yuma homes at that time, the NELS:88 data suggest that Cibola's demand for high expectations was right on target. Jon Walk, Jim Sullivan, and the whole Cibola staff were unknowingly responding to the latent expectations of their entering eighth graders.

BEGINNING WITH HIGH EXPECTATIONS

In 1988, after more than a year spent planning, traveling, attending conferences, and interviewing and hiring teachers, Jon Walk opened Cibola High School as its first principal. According to the current principal, Tony Steen, Walk laid the groundwork for Cibola by visualizing "a school that felt like a happy family where all students would be expected to succeed." Those aspirations were translated into school practices that drove a demanding curriculum and reflected the high expectations of the staff, teachers, and students. A science teacher explained:

[T]he state standards focus on biology, earth science, [and] physical science. . . . So . . . [when] they come into their freshman team and take biology, there isn't a low-level option. [T]hey come in and they do the biology or the biology honors.

A girl who had recently transferred as a sophomore to Cibola and said she was now working hard to bring her 2.6 GPA up to her former 3.8 commented, "The work . . . they explain [it] a lot better. There's more work to do here; they ask you for things like research papers. Over there [at her former high school], I don't remember doing a research paper at all." Her words were echoed by a boy who had arrived at Cibola as an

English learner the previous year and was now in honors English: "They encourage you, they challenge you, they push you up to the next level—that's what's helped me a lot."

The school's high standards appear to promote an atmosphere of success for everyone where being a good student is desirable and expected. As one student said, "It's cool to do well [at Cibola]. It's very competitive for seniors."

Another student compared CHS to her former school and explained:

> [S]chool is more important here than over there. . . . [Y]ou see students caring more for school here. . . . [P]eople in your own classroom, they challenge you to do more stuff; you have more supportive friends. . . . [O]ver there, they just give you the stuff and if you want to do it or not . . . well . . . here you're more encouraged to do it.

We already know that the founding staff at Cibola was determined to "take the lid off." They believed that the students at their former schools had not been expected to succeed. Indeed, some of the incoming Cibola counselors had been frustrated because counseling at their former schools had been reserved for those students who appeared to be "worthy" of the effort. The rest, most of them poor and minority students, were lucky to receive the minimal attention allotted to them.

Jon Walk had shared his colleagues' frustrations. He had a strong sense of efficacy and believed "that schools are for kids, and that we can make a difference in the life of kids, both academically and socially. The school was built on the philosophy that we would make a difference, that we would help kids be successful." In that statement, Jon Walk expressed his own sense of efficacy as well as his belief in the power of high expectations. Those two closely related ideas have a lot to do with Cibola's success in the early years and also with the school's ability to sustain that success over many years and through many changes. In the next few paragraphs, we will take a look at those ideas and their influence on Cibola's history.

EFFECTIVE SCHOOLS

Although high expectations are now considered an essential component of a good educational environment, it was not always that way. Back in the 1960s, the Coleman Report, an influential government-sponsored research project, concluded that educational achievement was largely independent of a child's experiences in school. According to Coleman, families and friends, not schools, had the most influence on achievement.[2]

Coleman's conclusions were controversial, to say the least. Although the report's unflinching documentation of the wide discrepancies found in the lives and education of children of different races, ethnicities, and socioeconomic classes was applauded, the report's conclusions were challenged on technical grounds by several researchers. Others welcomed a report that confirmed their own beliefs, and used them to back up their own low opinion of the schools.

Coleman's report also led many challengers to ask: If schools could not make a difference, then what was the reason for the consistent achievement differences found among groups of children? The controversy became an important topic for several years as educational researchers attempted to answer that question. While some blamed the families and the ethnic/racial characteristics of the children for their low achievement, others believed that hereditary factors exerted the major influence, and still others blamed social and economic disparities for the difference.

In the midst of this controversy, a group in the United Kingdom began a study that was intended to clarify the weight of the various influences on children's learning at the secondary school level. Rutter and colleagues conducted a longitudinal study comparing 12 secondary schools located within a large area of inner London.[3] In this case, the students were followed from entry through the completion of secondary school so the researchers were able to compare student performance before secondary school and then each year until graduation.

Their data uncovered important differences in both the behavior and achievement of the students across the different schools. This was true even when comparisons were restricted to children who entered the school with similar family and personal characteristics. In their conclusions, published in 1979, these researchers argued for the power of what they called an overall school "ethos" —that is, the spirit of a culture or a community as manifested in its organization's beliefs and aspirations.

Secondary schools are like other social organizations, they explained, and as such each school tends to develop its own set of general attitudes, culture, and patterns of behavior. Schools varied, for example, in the ways they dealt with disciplinary problems, and in the norms and values they established regarding student work and behavior. Specific actions to emphasize academic expectations played their part: "Children are liable to work better if taught in an atmosphere of confidence that they will succeed in the tasks they are set."[4]

In the United States, the vigorous reaction generated by Coleman's conclusion that "schools didn't make a difference" had an unexpected positive impact. It led to the development of a body of research that became the basis for the Effective Schools movement.

Dr. Ron Edmonds, then director of the Harvard Center for Urban Studies, was among those who took exception to the conclusions of the Coleman Report, as well as to the compensatory education programs that followed.[5] He believed that those programs focused on changing students' behavior in order to compensate for their disadvantaged backgrounds while making no effort to change the schools' behavior. In response to what they thought were inappropriate assumptions, a number of educational researchers, led by Edmonds and his colleague Larry Lezzote, conducted research supporting the premise that *all* children can learn and that the school controls the factors necessary to ensure student mastery of the core curriculum.

The first task undertaken by the effective schools researchers was to locate elementary schools that were successful in educating all students regardless of their socioeconomic status, ethnicity, or family background. They found such schools in various locations in both large and small communities. They then tried to identify the common characteristics among the effective schools. Those attributes were formally identified by Ron Edmonds as the "Correlates of Effective Schools" in a 1982 paper entitled "Programs of School Improvement: An Overview." Edmonds stated that all effective schools had:

- The leadership of a principal notable for substantial attention to the quality of instruction
- A pervasive and broadly understood instructional focus
- An orderly, safe climate conducive to teaching and learning
- Teacher behaviors that convey the expectation that all students are expected to obtain at least minimum mastery
- The use of measures of pupil achievement as the basis for program evaluation.[6]

The Effective Schools movement did not totally discount the important impact of family and socioeconomic standing on student learning. In the paper mentioned above, Edmonds also noted that "while schools may be primarily responsible for whether or not students function adequately in school, the family is probably critical in determining whether or not students flourish in school."[7]

LOW SOCIAL CAPITAL DOES NOT MEAN LOW ASPIRATIONS

Although families are important, they should not be used as an excuse for the underachievement of poor children. It is certainly true that the social capital available to middle- and upper-class children, of whatever ethnicity, provides a major benefit to them when they enter school. However, a lack of family resources should not be confused with lack of aspirations by less well-off students or their parents. Aspirations to higher education have, in fact, been on the increase, as can be seen in Figure 2.1.

In a 2001 longitudinal study (80 children from kindergarten through 6th grade), Goldenberg and colleagues challenged the notion that Latino(a) parents, due to their own experience with discrimination and resulting lack of faith in the instrumental value of schooling, had lower aspirations and expectations for their children.[8]

Goldenberg and his colleagues found instead that (at least through 6th grade) the achievement of children was not constrained by their parents' low educational expectations or aspirations. They found that even when a child's performance was not stellar, parents would modify their

Figure 2.1. Percent of High School Seniors Expecting to Attain a Bachelor's Degree or Attend Graduate/Professional School, by Family Socioeconomic Status (SES).

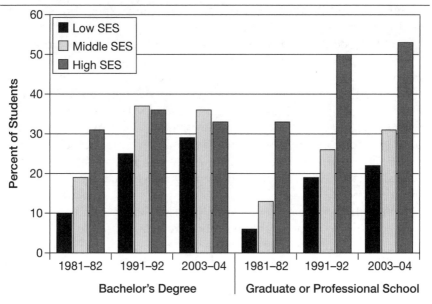

expectations but not their aspirations. As the researchers emphasize: "This is an important finding, because educators often cite low parental expectations and aspirations as part of the explanation for the generally low educational performance of children of Latino immigrants."[9] Lacking that excuse, the need for interventions directly aimed at the improvement of teaching and learning in schools becomes even more important.

Although many late-20th-century studies (e.g, Rutter et al., 1979; Edmonds, 1982) found a strong connection between high expectations and student achievement, particularly for minority students, only recently have leading educational reform entities strongly embraced high expectations as the baseline upon which to build their 21st-century reform efforts. Achieve,[10] for example, launched its Diploma Project in 2005 in order to "close the expectations gap and better prepare students for college and the workplace" (see, www.achieve.org/theexpectationsgap2010). Similarly, the Pathways to College Network extends the notion of high expectations beyond the school and affirms that,

> Education leaders must champion a compelling vision of high expectations within their states, districts, schools, and communities. Teachers, counselors, parents, and community stakeholders alike must believe that all students are capable of achieving at high levels and that all must be prepared to succeed in postsecondary education and work.[11]

But the question remains: How are those high expectations instantiated in the school setting? How are they sustained? And, for the purposes of this book, how did this approach get so ingrained at Cibola?

Those who promote high expectations usually give the following advice to schools: Tell students that you're expecting a lot from them. Present them with a challenging program and encourage them to do more. Good advice, but we all know that it is not easy to communicate high expectations and that students are very good at detecting false notes in a teacher's voice. Also, there is always that underlying, but seldom spoken, doubt: How much can a teacher really do for students whose parents don't have the educational background to offer their children the support of their families?

Although high expectations are always at the top of any list of recommendations for those pursuing school reform, these are some of the reasons why such expectations are hard to implement and harder even to identify. So what can be done? Cibola provides one example of how expectations for individual students have been built into and thrive within a schoolwide culture of high expectations.

A SENSE OF EFFICACY

Once again, Jon Walk helps us understand how that happened at Cibola:

> We had high expectations for students. . . . But most places just
> leave it at that. We [also] had high expectations for the staff. We
> had high expectations for the teachers. . . .When teachers make
> that part of their belief system, then they have high expectations
> of their students. But if the teachers have high expectations of
> their students but not of themselves, it doesn't happen. That's
> what you're going to see in most of the schools today. The teach-
> ers do have high expectations of their students, but not of them-
> selves. . . . [Y]ou have to have high expectations of your staff and if
> they accept that and believe that, then they understand that [this
> is] the only way that you can legitimately have high expectations,
> and high outcomes, from the students.

That is, "you have to believe in your own power to raise students' capacity to achieve."

The connection between teachers' belief in their own ability to effect
change in their students has been called a teacher's sense of efficacy. This
important component of the process is seldom addressed in discussions
about school reform. Yet, according to Bandura,

> Teachers with a high sense of instructional efficacy operate on the belief
> that difficult students are teachable through extra effort and appropriate
> technique and that they can enlist family supports and overcome negating
> community influences through effective teaching. In contrast, teachers who
> have a low sense of instructional efficacy believe there is little they can do if
> students are unmotivated.[12]

THE CHALLENGE

Cibola's teachers faced the challenge of a large, mostly poor, and in many
cases non–English speaking population. Few of their students' parents
were college graduates, and many had not even finished high school. In
fact, even today, more than 20 years after Cibola's opening, Yuma is sixth
among towns in the United States with the lowest levels of BA completion.[13] That is significant because, as the NCES study indicated, parental
level of education has been identified as one of the major influences on

students' expectations for themselves: "High school graduates whose parents did not go to college tend to report lower educational expectations than their peers as early as eighth grade."[14] But that should not be interpreted as "low aspirations." It is more likely to reflect parental lack of information about what is possible for their children, given their low levels of schooling and income.

Levels of parental education have been consistently associated with high school completion and advanced schooling as well.[15] Sadly, this relationship was statistically demonstrated in 1994 when the NCES study took another look at the 1988 students we discussed earlier, the ones who had such high expectations for themselves. They found that among those children, the ones whose parents held a bachelor's degree or higher were more likely to select an academic high school program and to enroll in a postsecondary program. As a result, those 1988 high expectations were probably not realized for about one-third of the participants in those studies—specifically those whose parents lacked advanced education, as is clearly shown in Figure 2.2.

The differences that affect students' progression in schooling, be they income or education, correlate with differences in race or ethnicity. As reflected in Table 1.1, Native Americans, Blacks, and Latinos(as) are more likely to be poor and to have less formal education. Those differences have a major effect on their children as they progress through school. Poor, less formally educated parents are unable to provide their children with a quality preschool education or with the cultural activities available to the middle- and upper classes. Nor, as shown in Figure 2.2, can they successfully guide them through the steps necessary to enroll in postsecondary institutions. That is where the Cibola Way comes in.

THE CIBOLA WAY TO HIGH EXPECTATIONS

The two-thirds of the staff drawn from the two existing Yuma secondary schools were well aware of the conditions their students faced at home. They knew that most of their students' parents did not have the advanced schooling necessary to provide their children with models and guidance, not because they had low aspirations for them, but because they didn't have the experiences necessary to guide them, and their schools were not providing what was needed to fill those gaps.

The Yuma high school teachers who chose to move to Cibola had been working with local students for several years, and they were frus-

Figure 2.2. Relationship Between Parents' Highest Level of Education and Students' Postsecondary Attainment (data from NCES '94).

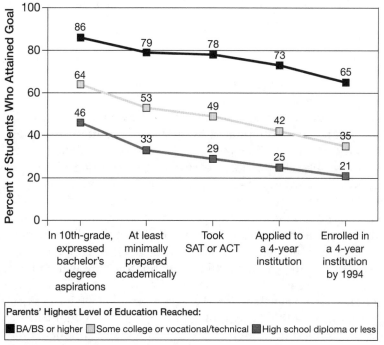

Parents' Highest Level of Education Reached:
■ BA/BS or higher ☐ Some college or vocational/technical ■ High school diploma or less

trated. Too few of their students were succeeding and too many were dropping out. When the new school was proposed and Jon Walk was selected to lead it, those teachers and counselors were ready for a change.

So the Cibola staff set high expectations for their students and, in so doing, they also set high expectations for themselves: "You're going to go to college." Walk says, "We made believers out of them [the students] by talking about it, by exposing them to the Preliminary SAT, by bringing in the scholarship programs [trading a teacher position for a scholarship seeker position]."

All of these things, he says, got the students thinking that maybe they could go to college, that maybe there was a way. He continues, "I think our high expectations for students was really looking at the goal: let's Let's go to college. . . . [W]e tried to focus on that. So why do all of this work, why do all of this reading, why be a good thinker, why does all of this matter? Well, it matters because 4 years later you can go on to further education."

Walk concludes that what made high expectations work for Cibola was the combination of having high expectations for the students plus having the staff have high expectations for themselves. Bandura might say that those teachers, and indeed all of the Cibola staff, had high levels of instructional expectancy for their students as well as for themselves.

COLLECTIVE EFFICACY

The words spoken by those in the original leadership staff at Cibola High School leave no doubt about the high expectations that they, and their faculty, brought to the new school. By the time Cibola opened, the high sense of self-efficacy noted earlier had been broadened to include their new colleagues. A sense of collective efficacy had developed. Each of them knew that they had all been chosen on the basis of their high expectations not only for their students but also for themselves. As a faculty, they were all determined to "take the lid off," as Badone has said. They trusted one another to accomplish the goals they had in common. They also understood that the higher standards they were advocating would need to be backed up with learning activities that were structured and conducted in ways that would ensure mastery. As Bandura has said, "High standards will not accomplish much, and can actually be demoralizing, unless learning activities are structured and conducted in ways that ensure they will be mastered."[16]

Cibola's brand-new faculty did not disappoint. I have found their continued insistence on high expectations to be not only the most basic component of the school's success but also its ground. But saying that you have high expectations expresses only a hope, and hopes are often dashed in the day-to-day realities of most schools. This does not seem to happen often in Cibola's case. Perhaps because before the school opened officially, the Cibola faculty had planned some ways to communicate their high expectations to the students.

They already had their mission statement displayed in every classroom, but that was not enough. They knew that most of their students were coming from poor homes with hard-working parents who had limited opportunities to advance their education and less money to make further education a reality. So they visited the sending schools and spoke to their soon to be students and their parents.

They firmly believed that their students were capable of going beyond high school and they trusted in their students' parents to support those goals. They encouraged the incoming classes to begin thinking and planning what they wanted to do after graduation because they were going to go beyond high school. High school was only a step toward the life they wanted, not the end of schooling, Sullivan and Luján told them. They also spoke to their students' parents. They told them that not only could their children go to college, but also that the Cibola staff would be there to ensure that they had the financial help necessary to make that possible.

The high expectations that welcomed the students arriving on the first day of school in September 1988 were not only academic but also behavioral, silently communicated by the closed campus they entered.

A CLOSED CAMPUS

The decision to close the campus began as a solution to a problem, but it appears to have had a major influence on the culture of the school. Cibola was surrounded by farmland when it opened. Unlike the locations of the other two Yuma high schools, there were no vendors close by and, since the students were only freshmen or sophomores, few of them could drive to more distant locations.

There were also concerns with safety and security. According to Gary Wiersema, who was vice principal at the time, many parents were concerned about sending their children to what was then all the way out to a different, largely undeveloped part of town. They wanted their children to learn, but they wanted them to be protected while away from home. For all those reasons, the campus was closed and the school was designed with a kitchen and dining area large enough to accommodate the total student population. This was just fine for Walk and Wiersema, both of whom had experienced the difficulties of monitoring student populations at schools with open campuses.

According to Wiersema, there was also a certain satisfaction in doing things differently at Cibola. After all, he says,

> It was made clear to everyone that came to work at Cibola that this was a new beginning. At no time did we want to hear how things were done previously at another school. We were not looking back, only forward. It was important to us to monitor our students without worrying about the influence or actions of "non-students" on our campus.

The parents were, of course, pleased to have the students under supervision rather than running around town, but the students, as expected, resisted. They wanted to have an open campus, just like the other high schools. To advance the process of acceptance of the inevitable, the Cibola staff made a conscious effort to offer food options that were similar to those found off campus and allowed students to move throughout the courtyard to find relaxing places to eat. "Visibility during the lunch hour by all staff members was essential to reducing problems," says Gary Wiersema. "We monitored every lunch hour, walked around and talked with all the students, ate lunch with them, picked up any piece of paper we found on the floor or in the courtyard to let kids know they were important to us and to show the pride we had in our school. When a problem did happen, we were there immediately to take care of it."

The closed campus also eliminated some peripheral problems, such as students returning to class late or not at all or having to deal with problems arising beyond the campus. Thus, the closed campus provided the first of the many strategies that were adopted by the school through the years in the effort to create a favorable culture for learning and maximizing instructional time. From this perspective, it may also have helped to create a bond between students and teachers, who were all together within that fenced environment, while also promoting a sense of continuity to the school day.

It is interesting to note that the advantages that high schools derive from closed campuses have made them quite popular recently. After years of open campuses, the trend is going back to closed campuses, which are favored by 71% of the public. Today, all the high schools in Yuma operate within closed campuses.[17]

OPENING DAY

As noted earlier, the students assigned to Cibola were drawn from two sides of town: the West Side and Sommerton. They didn't know each other because they attended different middle schools, but that didn't keep them from holding enmity towards the "other." We have already briefly noted the difficulties that arose on the first day of school, remembered as "a white-knuckles day" by former vice principal Wiersema. Not only were the West-siders and the Sommerton kids facing each other for the first time, but the buses dropped their charges off a full 40 minutes before the school was to be officially opened. The students began to line up across from each other as they arrived from their opposite sides of town. This was a tense moment and also a rigorous test for the staff. There was a limit to how much self-control they could expect from these neighborhood gangs that had never happily shared the same space before, let alone a new schoolyard. And they had to hold the peace for 40 minutes.

The administrators didn't wait. Every adult in the school was summoned. They did not shout warnings or threaten disciplinary action. Instead, they walked around the students and interacted informally with them. Gradually, friendly but guarded adults established their benevolent authority over their new students. That scene was repeated every day, with decreasing tension, until the schedule was adjusted in the spring semester. During that whole period, the key, says Gary Wiersema, was visibility. As teachers and administrators hovered around their more than 900 freshmen and sophomores, they all got to know each. By the end of the first year, the top administrators knew every one of the students by name. The incident also provided the first test for Cibola's high expectations. In this case, the school's expectations for civil behavior regardless of circumstances.

THE GUIDANCE OFFICE

Cibola's first students soon learned that a guidance office devoted to helping them create their future backed up what they had heard from the counselors who had visited their schools. One of those visiting counselors was Jim Sullivan (Sully), Jon Walk's former colleague and his choice to head the guidance office. According to Jon, "Sully deserves more credit for Cibola than [I do]."

The guidance office was set up to carry out the ambitious goals that Cibola was setting for itself. From the beginning, by turning a teaching position into a "scholarship specialist" and requiring students to create 4-year plans, the student's gaze was directed beyond high school. They were also provided with concrete ways to begin making decisions to reach the future they visualized for themselves.

The curriculum was based on college entrance requirements from the beginning. It also included classes for more advanced students. That was something Walk didn't want at the beginning because it often leads to a multitiered student population. But the faculty was able to come to an agreement. The classes would be offered but acceptance into those classes would depend on one of the following criteria: The students' grades, their parents' wishes, or—and this was what Walk required—the students' own choice. Thus, at Cibola, access to advanced classes would be open to any student willing to do the required work.

In 1988, Cibola was far ahead of the trend to offer honors and AP classes at schools with similar demographics. And the school is still ahead of the pack regarding who gets admitted to those classes. Many schools continue to predetermine, on the basis of grades, tests, or teacher recommendations, the makeup of those classes—a process that often leads to the obvious within-school segregation that has been so well documented by Sacks.[18]

Cibola's high expectations for their students were also reflected in their protection of instructional time. As you walk around campus, you notice the silence that is only broken by the brief periods between classes. That is because the public announcement (PA) system is used only once during the school day, in the morning for announcements and the communal pledge of allegiance, and instruction is never interrupted during the first 35 minutes of class time. Not even the counselors can break the "35-minute rule." They need to wait, as does everyone else, to allow teachers to get their classes under way without interruption.

All of these policies, Jon Walk says, "made believers out of them [the students] by talking about it, by exposing them to the pre-SAT, by bringing in the scholarship programs [and changing the teacher position into a scholarship-seeker position]. All of these things started to [affect] the view of the students: 'Maybe I should go to college, maybe there is a way.' I think our high expectations for students were really a way to look at the goal: Let's go to college." And Sully adds, "Or to other post–high school training programs."

Chapter Three

Leadership

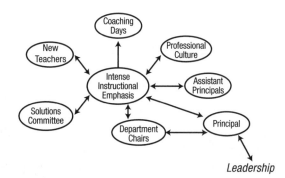

Leadership

Thousands of books and research articles have explored the role the principal plays in student achievement, especially in a large high school such as Cibola. As discussed in the last chapter, both Edmonds and Rutter and colleagues argued that the principal played a very important role in student achievement.[1] Around the same time, Murphy, after a thorough review of the literature on principal leadership, failed to find proof of the principal's contribution to learning outcomes.[2] So the question remains: What is leadership, and how does the principal, as the school's leader, influence student achievement?

I begin this chapter with a discussion about Jon Walk's leadership and how the pattern he set has been sustained by those who followed him in that role. We will examine how each of them, as principals, sustained the ideals upon which Cibola was built while also adding to the school's effectiveness.

THEORIES OF LEADERSHIP

The concept of leadership has given rise to many theories, books, and definitions. One of my favorites is credited to Alan Keith of Genentech: "Leadership is ultimately about creating a way for people to contribute to making something extraordinary happen."[3] That quote is particularly well suited to Jon Walk's approach to his potential role as the new principal of Cibola High School. Recall that Walk was feeling frustrated within the confines of a school that, he had realized, did not expect very much from its students, particularly from its Latino(a) students. He believed that they could accomplish much more, and he also knew that many of his colleagues felt the same way he did, especially Jim (Sully) Sullivan, to whom Walk gives special credit for Cibola's success.

Sully was the first head of guidance at Cibola, and under his leadership, the office became the heart of the school. We will discuss this topic at length in the next chapter.

THE PRINCIPAL'S EXPECTATIONS

How much did Walk's high expectations contribute to Cibola's accomplishments? We know that as soon as he was selected to lead the new school, more than a year before the school opened, Walk went into action. He proclaimed to all who would listen his intention to run a school where every student would be expected to achieve and not only graduate, but continue on to further education. That was all many of his friends and colleagues needed. They, too, were eager to accomplish something extraordinary. They, too, believed in their students' capacity to go beyond high school. So they joined him. So many teachers volunteered that it was necessary for some of them to wait until the following year. At that time additional grades would be added, thus opening up more teaching positions.

Walk was ready. He was one of those exceptional leaders described by Hargreaves and Fink who, from the first day of his appointment, thought hard about how he might implement deep, broad, and long-lasting reforms.[4] Walk was already familiar with the principal's role. His father was a school principal, and Jon had been exposed to life in schools as seen from the principal's office: "I knew that I always wanted to be a principal, and I knew what I wanted to do when I was a principal." I asked him what that was, and he explained:

> Selecting the very best people possible, I think that's still number one. Hire the very best people possible because it is a lot easier to select great people and help them stay great than it is to select people that aren't great and try to make them great. . . . To go along with that is to provide these great people with guidance; provide them with freedom; provide them with the knowledge that, if they make a mistake, that would be okay; provide them with the opportunity to be leaders themselves within areas of the school. I think that's probably the philosophy we built on. Along with the philosophy everybody seemed to buy into that we're here to make this the best school that we can make. *That was number one on the table for us.*

As noted earlier, *leadership* is defined in many different ways, and for each definition there seems to be an illustrative metaphor. Beck and

Murphy, scholars in educational administration, identified the variety of dominant metaphors applied to school administrators in the United States across the years.[5] From the "Values Broker" of the 1920s to the "Instructional Leader" of the 1980s, different metaphors seemed to arise to capture the essence of each decade's conception of the principal's role.

Beck and Murphy's book was published in the early 1990s, shortly after Cibola's opening, so they could not predict what dominant metaphors might arise in the future. However, they identified metaphors for leadership that were then emerging and proposed several that they thought might be applied to principals in the 1990s and beyond. One of those metaphors, the "Principal as Servant," resonates with many of Jon Walk's statements above and in earlier chapters, as well as with comments made about him by those who chose to follow him to Cibola.

THE PRINCIPAL AS SERVANT

Robert K. Greenleaf first proposed the metaphor of the principal as servant in 1977. "It begins," he wrote, "with the natural feeling that one wants to serve. Then conscious choice makes one aspire to lead. . . . The difference between the servant-first and the leader-first is manifested in the care taken by the servant-first to make sure that other people's highest priority needs are being served."[6] According to Greenleaf, the best test of servant leadership is to see whether "those [who are] served grow as persons; do they, while being served, become healthier, freer, more autonomous, more likely themselves to become servants?"[7] Toni Badone says that Jon Walk "made" leadership; he made it easy for people to become leaders. Walk encouraged them, Badone says, "by truly giving people the courage to be whatever it was they were going for, maybe even to think about it when they had not yet considered that possibility."

HOW IS WALK REMEMBERED?

Every member of Jon Walk's original staff I have interviewed credit him not only for Cibola's success, but also for the encouragement that led them to take on larger responsibilities. Toni Badone, quoted above, remembers when she was a teacher and Walk asked her whether she had thought about becoming an administrator. She responded that she had, "a long time ago, but I have four kids now," to which he responded, "What difference does it make? You're a teacher; you have certain headaches. I'm an administrator; I have certain headaches. You just trade one set of headaches for another set." She adds: "He just moved the obstacles out of the way and gave people the courage to do what needed to be done."

Tony Steen knew Jon Walk long before he applied for the teaching position at the yet to open Cibola High School. He remembers, and continues to live, and act as Cibola's principal, following Jon's words:

> He talked about that kind of philosophy that we're a family, we're working, and we will accomplish a lot of things. If we work together as a family we're going to get these things done. It may be harder and it may be more difficult to do, but it's in the best interests of the kids. If we work as a team, as a family, we can get it done.

Steen's recollection of Walk's words fits another attribute of Greenleaf's servant-leader: the need to have an effect beyond the organization. "[W]hat is the effect on the least privileged in society; will he benefit or, at least, will he not be further deprived?"[8]

Gary Wiersema, who was Walk's assistant for administration, and, later, the second principal of Cibola, recalls his experience interviewing teachers with Walk in the Midwest:

> The basic foundation we wanted was high-energy, creative teaching. You have to like kids and [to want to] do whatever it takes for them to be successful. In return, as administrators, we would do everything we could to create the best possible learning environment, as well as doing whatever it takes for the teachers to be successful in their jobs of educating kids.

Notice that at the outset, before the school had opened, these administrators committed themselves to doing everything in their power to *serve* so that their teachers could be successful and, in turn, their students could succeed.

Jon Walk himself recalls his interviews with potential teachers in the Midwest. He presented them with a challenge: "[We're] going to be able to make a difference in a community that has a lot of students who have a lot of potential but [whose] potential hasn't been quite tapped yet. . . . [We're] going to tap it."

MORE THAN 20 YEARS LATER

What is most interesting about this story is that, after more than 20 years, these beliefs and expectations continue to be the base upon which Cibola operates, as is evident in the following comments from teachers whom I interviewed at the school. I asked Gary, who had taught at many different schools before coming to Cibola, whether and how Cibola differed from those other schools. He said:

> The ethnic makeup of the school is a lot different . . . but I think the main difference is that the administration at CHS has always allowed teachers opportunities to expand and to bring in a lot of new ideas and to try a lot of things as ways to get to the kids.

He then added:

> Every year, the educational leaders of the school get together and spend a day planning . . . and setting goals for the year and what they want to accomplish. They take some time to highlight what has worked and . . . the good aspects of the school. Like celebrating successes, which I think is a really great thing to do. And then they take a look at what [they] would like to improve upon.

According to Beck and Murphy, school principals as servant-leaders would use professional expertise and a moral imperative rather than line authority as their base of influence, learning to lead by empowering others rather than by controlling them.[9] This characteristic of Cibola's early leadership is evident in Cibola teacher Carol's response regarding what may account for the differences at CHS:

> [T]the administrators . . . set the standards and then let teachers operate within them [autonomously]. . . . They're expected to write lesson plans but don't have to turn them in, which to me means they trust us. They know we're doing our job, they know we're making lesson plans. . . . I have friends who are teachers in other schools, and this is a big area that they're spending a lot of time on. . . . They feel frustrated; they're wasting their time; they don't feel valued as professionals. . . . I think here, at this school, that makes a big difference. They treat everyone with respect, but yet they're firm about certain things. If someone is not doing their job they call them in.

Gary concludes that one of the things that makes the school successful is how the teachers encourage students and do not give up on them: "There are a lot of us that really work with the kids on their grades and encourage them, find ways to help them and not let them slip through."

COLLECTIVE TEACHER EFFICACY

What you hear in these teachers' voices is a sense of collective efficacy through which teachers believe not only in their own effort but also have the confidence that the efforts of the faculty, as a whole, will have a positive effect on students and promote an academic emphasis in the school.[10]

The high standards expected of all teachers hired at Cibola continue to be in evidence. Tony Steen, one of Walk's heirs and Cibola's current principal, commented on his reasons for replacing one of several newly hired teachers: "He was an experienced teacher, (but) he just couldn't handle it. He didn't like the way we do things. . . . [H]e had to work too hard . . . and he didn't want to work that hard. . . . [W]e offered all kinds of help, but it was best that he left; we didn't discourage him because he was unhappy, and we weren't going to be happy with him."

These high standards for teachers as well as for students continue the tradition set by Jon Walk and his administrative team. It's what is sometimes referred to as another example of "the Cibola Way," which resembles the sort of moral community proposed by Sergiovanni.[11]

THE SCHOOL AS A MORAL COMMUNITY

Sergiovanni argues for building the school on a covenant of shared values, and has offered a set of characteristics for what the covenant of a virtuous school might include. Among them are: 1) becoming a learning community; 2) believing that every student can learn and doing everything possible to ensure that every student does learn; 3) taking responsibility for doing everything in the school's power to attend to the developmental, physical, and social needs of its students and relying on an ethic of caring as a key to academic success; 4) honoring mutual respect across all levels; 5) bringing parents, teachers, the community, and the school together as partners with reciprocal and interdependent rights and obligations.[12] All of these characteristics, as we have seen, could be applied to Cibola.

Sergiovanni brings the two metaphors together when he concludes: "In the virtuous school, the leader would be seen as servant."[13] And that is, of course, how Walk and latter Cibola principals have considered their relationship with their teachers. They are there to serve their teachers, thus enabling the teachers to serve their students.

Servant leadership, from Beck and Murphy's perspective, would also differ from more traditional styles of leadership by being less direct and more ethereal and enabling.[14] Compare the descriptions of the principal as servant with Walk's earlier quote about wanting "to provide" for his followers and help them "become leaders themselves." It is easy to see Walk assuming a servant leadership role as he developed and implemented his vision for Cibola High School.

THE TRANSFORMATIONAL PRINCIPAL

In seeking to help their followers become leaders, servant leaders are also seeking to transform them. This results in an overlap between servant-principal and a more recently popular metaphor, the transformational leader. The overlap between those two metaphors for leadership, servant and transformational, has been analyzed by Smith, Montagno, and Kuzmenko.[15]

In their critical analysis of the characteristics of transformational and servant leaders, Smith, Montagno, and Kuzmenko find many areas of overlap. Both theories attach a lot of importance to the leader's being open and accountable to others and modeling appropriate behavior at a high level of integrity and trust. In both cases, the interpersonal components of the work are given a lot of importance, and the needs of others have priority. Both of these models of leadership also have a future orientation and facilitate a shared vision.

The models diverge, according to these scholars, in their suitability for different contexts. They suggest that transformative leadership is better suited to institutions within a dynamic external environment where people are encouraged to innovate and to take initiative and risks. In such cases, they argue, the servant leadership model may lead to frustration because of the leader's desire to bend to the rights of others. Thus, they propose that the servant leadership model may be more appropriate when an organization enters the maturity stage and concern for employees and their personal growth becomes more significant for effective leadership.

In the case of Cibola, it appears that Jon Walk was able to provide both the impetus to drive the transformation that he and his followers envisioned, and the encouragement and affirmation necessary to promote innovation and creativity among his followers. The evidence suggests that those who followed him in the principal's office were also able to balance their roles as both servant and transformational leaders. Perhaps that was because his followers were so very ready to join Walk in making something "extraordinary" happen.

THE LEGACY

The sequence of leaders over Cibola's 20-year history (see Table 3.1) is unusual in that the school has been led by members of the original staff not only in the principal's office, but also, to a large extent, in the all-important guidance office. That continuity and stability has made it possible to sustain the Cibola philosophy.

Counselor Luján remembers how "Walk made believers of all of us. . . . He kept telling us that we were the best school that was ever put together in Yuma. . . . He had lots of great ideas, but he allowed people below him to make decisions. He didn't have to control everything." Luján thinks that's what made Walk an outstanding principal: "It is because we were involved in the decision-making that we still carry on with some of the same basic concepts."

Table 3.1. Sequence of Leadership 1991–2009

Years	Principal	Assistant Principal	Director of Guidance
1988–1989	Jon Walk	Gary Wiersema	James Sullivan
1989–1990	Jon Walk	Gary Wiersema	James Sullivan
1990–1991	Jon Walk	Gary Wiersema	James Sullivan
1991–1992	Gary Wiersema	Johnny Rico	James Sullivan
1992–1993	Gary Wiersema	Johnny Rico	James Sullivan
1993–1994	Gary Wiersema	Johnny Rico	James Sullivan
1994–1995	Johnny Rico	Toni Badone	James Sullivan
1995–1996	Johnny Rico	Toni Badone	James Sullivan
1996–1997	Toni Badone	Susie Alka	Debbie White
1997–1998	Johnny Rico	Toni Badone	Debbie White
1998–1999	Johnny Rico	Toni Badone	Debbie White
1999–2000	Johnny Rico	Toni Badone	Debbie White
2000–2001	Toni Badone	Tony Steen	Shirley Auza
2001–2002	Tony Steen	Jamie Sheldahl	Shirley Auza
2002–2003	Tony Steen	Jamie Sheldahl	Rebecca García
2003–2004	Tony Steen	Jamie Sheldahl	Rebecca García
2004–2005	Tony Steen	Faith Klostrelch	Rebecca García
2005–2006	Tony Steen	Faith Klostrelch	Rebecca García
2006–2007	Tony Steen	Faith Klostrelch	Rebecca García
2007–2008	Tony Steen	Tim Brienza	Rebecca García
2007–2009	Tony Steen	Tim Brienza	Rebecca García
2009–2010	Tony Steen	Tim Brienza	Rebecca García

Cibola High School celebrated the 20th anniversary of its opening in 2008. Five different principals have led the school during that period, all of them members of the original staff. Wiersema, who was Walk's assistant for administration, assumed the principalship, with Rico as his vice principal, when Walk became assistant superintendent of the Yuma Union High School District in 1991. Wiersema recalls that

> [T]he vision for Cibola was solid. Now it was up to me to carry out the details . . . a great opportunity to continue to improve the educational environment for our staff and students while adding my own personal stamp. . . . Things have to change if you want to continue to improve, but the vision for the school, staff, and students was the same.

Wiersema remained in that position for 3 years, managing Cibola's growth spurt, before returning to the Midwest in 1994. At that time, Rico, who had been heading the department of social studies since the school's opening, took over as principal until 2000. He hired Toni Badone as his assistant principal for academics. One of the big changes during that time was the adoption of the freshman teams strategy (which I cover in Chapter 7).

There was a brief interlude between 1996 and 1997 when Rico went to the district office as assistant superintendent and Toni Badone became interim principal at Cibola. Rico returned for the 1997–1998 school year and remained principal until 2000, with Badone as vice principal for academics. In 2000, he returned to the district office as assistant superintendent for personnel, and Toni Badone became Cibola's principal. She chose Tony Steen, then director of athletics, as her assistant principal for academics. In 2001, Badone became assistant superintendent for curriculum and Steen assumed Cibola's principalship.

STEEN'S PATH

Steen remembers being a bit apprehensive about accepting his appointment as the vice principal of academics, a position usually reserved for people from the academic areas. But, he says, "[Toni Badone] had confidence that I would do a very good job, and that gave me the confidence to do my best." As it turned out, he was soon to take even larger responsibilities. In 2001, Badone was named assistant superintendent for academics and Steen was appointed principal of Cibola, where he remains to this day.

Steen feels fortunate that both Rico and Badone were there to support him at the beginning whenever he needed help. Particularly because they really knew Cibola, and Steen wanted to remain faithful to the spirit and the policies that had been previously established.

Like Jon Walk, Steen is known for his visibility. He's out on campus in the morning, during class changes, and at dismissal. For 2 days every week, Ms. Dee Lux, his attentive secretary, clears his schedule for unannounced classroom visits. The visits are 10 to 20 minutes each and are followed by a brief note, a few comments, his thank you, and, if necessary, a request for the teacher to come and see him later. These visits and the mentoring program, which provides 2 years of support for all beginning teachers and experienced teachers who are new to Cibola, is how Tony Steen ensures the instructional quality that the school promises.

Steen has been the principal at Cibola since I began visiting the school in 2004. Although I have personally interviewed all of Cibola's past and present top administrators, I have only witnessed Steen occupying that chair. But his style and philosophy suggest that Jon Walk has left a large footprint on Cibola.

Steen recalls, "During the initial interview and teacher induction, the expectations and confidence given to the Cibola staff were that we would be successful if we all worked together to accomplish our goals. Family was the one term that seemed to permeate the campus." It is still alive and well today at Cibola.

Steen has already left his own mark on Cibola with the introduction of the tardy sweep and the increase from three AP courses and 4% participation in 2001 to ten AP courses and 18% participation in 2007. Furthermore, English learners, most of whom are native speakers of Spanish, can now benefit from taking AP Spanish. But perhaps Tony's most important contribution is his humanity, as reflected in counselor Luján's comment: "Our administrator, Mr. Steen, such a wonderful man. When we had open house, he was at the front of the auditorium shaking the hands of the new parents and their kids as they came in. How many principals do that?"

I believe that the continuity of the vision for the school held by its leaders is the main reason why Cibola High School has been able to beat the odds so consistently. For more than 20 years, the staff has been able to maintain the impetus that drove the school's success at the outset as well as develop policies that sustain their goals for the future. This consistency has led to the sustainability that has been found to be a key force in meaningful, long-term change.

In a study that followed 20 schools in Canada and the United States for 30 years, Hargreaves and Fink found that, with some exceptions, "[M]ost school leadership practices create temporary, localized flurries of change but little lasting or widespread improvement. Leadership succession was rarely successful as charismatic leaders were followed by less-dynamic successors who could not maintain the momentum of improvement."[16] But they did find a few exceptional leaders who, from the first day of their appointment, thought hard about how they might implement deep, broad, and long-lasting reforms.

I fully agree with these researchers' findings about the value of sustainability; I have seen it work at Cibola. However, I question the importance the researchers ascribe to "charismatic" leaders followed by "less-dynamic" ones.

I have interviewed all of the principals of Cibola and have met all but Wiersema, who lives in Indiana, in person. (I have spoken at length with him over the phone.) I would not describe any one of them as "charismatic." That characterization is much too shallow for Cibola's leaders. On the other hand, I have found all of them to be caring, thoughtful, persuasive, and hard-working. They persuade through the strength of their convictions, not through charm. None of Cibola's principals would be especially noticeable upon entering the room, and when speaking about Cibola, they are typically nonchalant about their contribution to its success. Much like Collins's good-to-great leaders, instead of talking about their accomplishments, they promptly divert your attention to the school's carefully selected, talented, and devoted teachers. Maybe that is why Cibola, unlike other supposedly successful schools, has managed to survive and improve through the years.

Chapter Four

Counseling and Guidance: The Heart of the School

Jon Walk argues that Jim Sullivan, or "Sully," is more deserving of credit for Cibola's success than he is. He's partly right. Sullivan's conception of the role of counseling and guidance has played a huge part in the school's success, but, of course, it was Jon Walk who asked Sullivan to head that department. Without diminishing Sully's extraordinary contribution to Cibola, we may wonder whether he would have been able to create his kind of guidance office at any other school, under any other principal. In fact, he had been at another school in the district for several years before Walk brought him to Cibola, but he had no influence there. That administration did not believe, as Walk and Sully did at Cibola, that their students could be college material.

ASSERTIVE GUIDANCE

At Cibola, Sully was supported by a principal who, like him, deeply believed that all their students had a high potential for success and that what I would call "assertive guidance" could help them reach their goals. Walk shared Sully's frustrations about the assumptions being made about Yuma's students, so he gave Sully license, as head of guidance, to do whatever he felt was necessary to ensure that Cibola's graduates not only finished high school but went as far as they wanted to go beyond that.

Jim Sullivan was very ready for that responsibility. He had spent 4 years in Mexico after completing both BA and MS degrees in Spanish and confessed to "having a passion for the people and for the language." After 15 years of teaching Spanish at one of the other Yuma high schools,

Sullivan realized that there were no Spanish-speakers in the counseling office to help the newcomers. He thought they deserved as much or more help as anybody else in the district, so he went back to school to get his counseling degree and went into counseling as a way to do something meaningful as well as apply his Spanish skills.

Sully believed in kids and in what they were capable of achieving. But it had been difficult to act on those sentiments as a counselor at his previous school. Walk recognized Sully's value and gave him the opportunity to create a brand new guidance office. In Walk's words, "When we got down there and we put him in charge he just blossomed, he took off with that role."

THE HEART OF THE SCHOOL

Walk believes that Sully saw his new position as a grand opportunity to affect students, perhaps thinking "I can affect the life of every single kid because of the fact that I supervise all the counselors. I have this kinship with the administrators and they have given me the license that is necessary to make this place work." Under Sully's stewardship, the guidance office became a place where students came first and every one of them was expected, and helped, to succeed.

With Walk as his principal, Sully was able to negotiate a relationship based on trust that ensured independence for the guidance office. Geralyn Weil, another of Walk's early picks for counselor, remembers how "Sully negotiated that counselors wouldn't have to do testing, that they could really focus on being counselors. The administration would run the school, but the counselors would actually make the decisions for the counseling office." She continued:

> [Walk] very, very strongly stated that he felt that the counselors were hired because they were good and competent and he didn't need to know everything so they should do what they did best. . . . He wanted us to do the things that we needed to do to build a good school and he gave us free rein.

The original counselors were Jim Sullivan, Geralyn Weil, Helen Rice, and Conrad Luján (who worked half-time the first year, full-time after that, and is still serving Cibola's students). They were the ones who welcomed Cibola's opening class of 978 freshmen and sophomores in 1988.

Sully proceeded to create a guidance office that is considered by everyone, past and present, to be the heart of the school. His main concern as a counselor was:

> not just get them to finish high school, because that's immaterial to me. [W]e never talk about just doing high school . . . we talk about . . . going on to postsecondary education. That's the whole key to everything. And if you can make the kids believe that, and truly believe that you're interested in them as a person. . . . I can't believe a person accepting mediocrity in their lives.

There you have the belief system that underlies the structure of Cibola's guidance office. So how do you instantiate such a belief system?

MAKING IT HAPPEN

You begin by assuming that every entering student is capable of pursuing studies beyond high school and you communicate that expectation to every entering class and their parents, well ahead of their arrival at Cibola. You also relieve everyone's fears about the unknown, especially about costs, by assuring them that resources will be available because the school and counselors can help. Trust in us, you say. Throughout their orientation period, students and parents keep hearing a consistent message from the counselors, the administrators, and their teachers.

Next, you give students a career survey to help them identify their areas of interest, their dreams, and their goals, and then ask them to fill out a 4-year plan that is compatible with those goals. Now, perhaps for the first time, students begin to see the connection between their school work and their goals and the path to get there. After a few weeks of such treatment, students begin to shift and broaden their goals. They begin to trust the adults and, most important, to believe in themselves. I believe Roderick had such a process in mind when she commented:

> [E]ducators must realize that preparation will not necessarily translate into access to college if high schools do not provide better structure and support for students in college search, planning, and application. . . . Students and their families need to believe that high aspirations are attainable. . . . [S]tudents "believe" when they feel well supported and capable of achieving their goal. . . . They also believe when their schools provide concrete structures and supports for college—so that students know they can rely on their school for information and guidance—and when their school demonstrates a track record of success.[1]

THE COUNSELOR'S ROLE

That is the broad outline of what Sully and the original counselors set in motion. Their system continues to this day, and gradually draws the students into a process that requires *the students* to think and plan for their futures. That is an important point.

Visiting the counselor is not an elective activity at Cibola. The new guidance office broke away from established traditions. The counselors did not sit and wait for the students to come calling on them. They went to their students instead and gave them the tools they needed so that, with professional help and assistance from their teachers, they could be the architects of their own futures. As far as I can tell, at that time (around 1988), and perhaps even now, Sully's model had no precedent in any public high school in the country. In fact, it was not too long ago when Arizona's superintendent of education, Tom Horne, proposed requiring all students to do what Cibola had been doing since 1988: Have every student develop a personal education plan. Apparently, he was not aware that this was already happening at Cibola High School in Yuma.

Unlike many public high school counselors in the late 1980s, Cibola's counselors were not there to serve only the "best" students and their parents. They were there to ensure that *all* students reached the goals they set for themselves beyond high school. Whether it was a 2- or 4-year college, trade school, or the military, a future orientation was what mattered.

You may recall our brief discussion in Chapter 2 about the first National Educational Longitudinal Study (NELS:88) of the academic expectations of eighth graders, conducted in 1988, coincidentally the same year Cibola opened. That study concluded that the vast majority of the students responding to the survey, regardless of race, ethnicity, or socioeconomic status (SES), aspired to go on to college. [2] Unfortunately, those high expectations were not realized for most of them. Follow-up studies to NELS:88 were conducted every 2 years until 1994—2 years beyond the completion of high school for the students in the study. Plank and Jordan's rigorous analysis of that data helps to explain what happened, or failed to happen, with those students between 1988 and 1994. [3]

TALENT LOSS

Plank and Jordan were especially interested in the problem of talent loss, defined as "the failure of high achieving students to enroll in

any type of postsecondary educational institution in the years immediately following high school."[4] They wanted to know why so many
students failed to achieve at the level of their aspirations, especially
students from the lower social classes who had demonstrated high
achievement.

Their analysis of the follow-ups revealed that talent loss was most se-
vere among students from the lowest socioeconomic backgrounds. They
found that "Even among high-achieving students, extreme talent loss
occurs among low-SES individuals at the point of transition from high
school."[5] In an effort to make the results of their study more concrete,
Plank and Jordan constructed four fictional case studies to illustrate their
findings.[6] The four cases are all assumed to be Black males with two
siblings from urban public schools who scored in the 75th percentile in
their prior test scores and are at the 50th percentile for SES. They are also
assumed to have requested financial support and to have applied to at
least one 2- or 4-year postsecondary institution.

The cases differ in the variables relating to guidance and preparation.
Case A represents an individual with a lot of social capital who has taken
many of the actions necessary to increase the chance that he will register in
a Public Educational Institution (PEI), especially a 4-year institution. Case
B, on the other hand, represents a student with little social capital who has
taken few of the actions necessary to help him get into a PEI. Case C represents an individual who benefits from a strong high school setting but
comes from a family that does not offer much information on postsecondary aspirations. Case D represents the reverse of Case C; he comes from a
strong family setting but a relatively weak high school setting.

The researchers then used the consecutive NELS data to determine
the probabilities that each of these fictional cases would reach the postsecondary level, given their profiles. They found that Case A, with his
high level of social capital, had about a 91% probability of enrolling in
a 4-year college and a very low probability of never enrolling. On the
other hand, Case B, who matched Case A in achievement and other background traits, was hampered by the lack of information, guidance, and
actions taken. As a result, Case B would have only a 50% chance of enrolling in a 4-year institution and a more than 27% chance of never enrolling. Cases C and D illustrated how family resources were somewhat
more important than school resources. Case D, who received strong family support while in a weak school setting, would have an almost 90%
chance of enrolling in a 4-year PEI. Case C, with strong school support
but weak family support, would have only a 75.8% chance of enrolling
in a 4-year PEI and an over 27% chance of never enrolling.

In their effort to understand the reasons for talent loss, the researchers were able to identify specific sources of information, guidance, and action that, when absent, served to explain the negative association between SES and talent loss. Those included communication and discussion among students, parents, and school personnel about academic matters and postsecondary preparation; encouragement to take the SAT or ACT; preparation for those tests; and actually taking the tests. When those aspects of information, guidance, and action were absent, the likelihood of postsecondary enrollment was decreased for children from low-income families.

In their conclusions, the researchers emphasize the importance of early and sustained efforts and warn that beginning the college advising program after the sophomore year may be too late. The researchers also recommend visits to colleges and exploration of the possibilities for financial aid. Many of these interventions, they conclude, point to the importance of social capital in facilitating transitions to postsecondary enrollment.

You have probably realized by now that what was put in place at Cibola in 1988 under Walk and Sullivan's leadership was just what Plank and Jordan recommended in 2000 following their research findings.

MAKING UP FOR LOW SOCIAL CAPITAL

"Talent loss" was a problem that Sullivan intuitively recognized, and one that he was determined to address at the time Cibola opened. Sullivan understood from his own experience as both a teacher and counselor what Plank and Jordan discovered through research. He knew what his students could do on their own and was also aware of the help they needed to compensate for the missing social capital others enjoyed. No time was wasted.

Early in the school's history, counselors at Cibola placed their emphasis on the perilous transition between middle school and high school. Several times during the year preceding Cibola's opening, Walk and Sullivan went to the sending schools to share the high expectations they held for the students coming to Cibola. They were expecting their students to go to college, and they offered help to get them there. That advance encouragement continues: Every year, Cibola's counselors meet with their incoming students at each of the sending middle schools. Counselor Luján says, "[W]e present this to all the kids in the auditorium (in both English and Spanish), here's our philosophy, here's what we expect from you. By the time we walk out [we ask], how many of you are going to go to college? And every hand goes up." But it was not always like that. A former middle school principal told me that the first year the Cibola counselors came to his school only a few of the incoming students would raise their hands, but it was not long before they all did. They had no idea what college was, but Sully saw that as part of the counseling team's responsibility, to teach them about college.

The strong encouragement is followed by the freshman orientation at Cibola when they arrive and continues with more guidance throughout the freshman year. Finally, the students take action by building their personal 4-year plan.

THE 4-YEAR PLAN

Cibola High School was the first public school in Yuma (perhaps in the nation) to develop and implement a 4-year plan. Students, with their counselors and teachers, decide on their intended educational/occupational direction and plan their 4 years of high school accordingly. There is plenty of room for change as they move along. Their plans are reviewed twice annually, but they need to keep moving towards their own chosen goal.

Teachers were enthusiastically supportive of the plan from the beginning, and they have willingly given up instructional time for this activity. The goal was, and is, to get the students to think about their futures so they can understand the importance of their coursework.

Students and parents are consistently advised that change is healthy and that the 4-year plan is a guide, with plenty of flexibility. As they move toward their senior year, the students become increasingly invested in their future. Cibola's success in sending most of its graduates (about 50% at the beginning, currently over 80%) on to higher education attests to the effectiveness of this process.

The 4-year plan is the center of everyone's attention during two of the most important days on the Cibola calendar: the biannual "credit checks." All counselors participate in these 2 days, which are devoted to ensuring that all students are progressing appropriately.

This is how the "credit checks" work: The counselors meet with all their seniors for about 4 or 5 days in August. The students are brought together by class periods (worked out ahead with their teachers) in a general assembly in the guidance office, where they watch an audiovisual presentation having to do with pre-graduation plans. Then, they are divided up and, in turn, each student goes to their counselor. The counselors spend a week working one-on-one with their seniors, informing the students of where they are and what they need, as well as making sure that their records are updated regarding their interests, what they want to do, and where they want to go to school next, and ensuring they have taken the appropriate steps to accomplish their goals (e.g., having taken the SAT and the ACT and passed the Arizona Instrument to Measure Standards test (AIMS). In the case of AIMS, students who have failed to meet the required level in a particular subject area (math, reading, writing) must take the appropriate classes so they so they can pass the test before graduation, a matter of particular concern for some students, especially English learners.

The counselors meet with the sophomores and the juniors in their classes (again, pre-arranged). In Becky García's words, "We take the show on the road, going from one class to another all day long for 5 to 6 days or however many days it takes." The counselors also supplement their comments with an audio-visual presentation that runs from 10 to 15 minutes and reminds the students of the need to keep up their records and to make sure they are taking the classes and tests they need for their particular future plan. The presentations are revised annually to ensure that they are up-to-date on the latest changes on requirements by the Board of Regents, the Board of Education, or the institutions to which they may be applying.

Sophomores and juniors also fill out a questionnaire regarding where they are in the number of credits approved, and where they want to continue their education. With the aid of the course catalog, they also begin to think about the electives they may want to take the following year. The counselors will then update their students' records and, when they meet with the students again in January or February, they return those responses to their students to verify whether their interests are still the same. "The counselors want to know whether what students said in October or September remains the same or if there is anything they want to change. They also want to know whether the students have any questions and if they expect any changes in their post-graduation plans

As Becky says,

[Y]ou know, kids . . . they never stay with one thing, which is okay. So that's what we do. . . . As counselors, we highlight the next level they need to go to and then they can tell us what electives they want. In other schools, they have a 4-year plan that's pre-designed. It's what they chose their freshman year. It's not giving them much flexibility. So . . . that's not going to work for this setting, for the philosophy of the department I work for, or for the team that I have. It's not going to work because we're in constant change. We have the flexibility. You know, maybe they weren't offering Ceramics II back when they were freshmen. Now they are, and they want to expand. . . . Maybe we weren't offering journalism, now we are. They want to take journalism.

THE OFFICE OF COUNSELING AND GUIDANCE

All of these counseling and guidance activities are directed from the office designed to be the most accessible one on campus. Unlike most of the guidance offices I have visited in other high schools, where the counselors are at the end of a hall or ensconced within a daunting administrative area, Cibola's guidance office is wide open to all visitors. The design was the result of a change made to the architectural plan submitted for the school. It was a deliberate move to make the guidance office the most easily accessible office in the school. It can be reached directly from the main campus, right across from the cafeteria, or from the official main school entry. This makes it easy for students and their parents to walk in unannounced and see the counselors directly without intervention from the administration. That, of course, results in many more interruptions for the counselors, but they accept that as the trade-off for increased accessibility.

Students hang out in the guidance area to peruse the latest Cibola news or to check out forms related to college and scholarship applications. The guidance area is where they wait to see their counselors, whose offices surround them against a backdrop of photographs of the previous year's scholarship winners. Behind that wall sits ever-patient Becky García, the current head of guidance, only a few steps away from the assistant principal for academics, who is responsible for constructing and overseeing the final schedule.

Ms. Becky

Rebecca (Becky) García was hired at Cibola in 1995, but she knew the school well already. She had been working for several years at the Arizona Western College (AWC), where she was in charge of putting on a program for students from area high schools every summer. Most of these students were from families whose parents had no experience with higher education. The idea was to help first-generation high school students prepare for college. Every summer, Becky tried to convince 30 students from each high school to participate in the summer program.

Cibola was one of the schools she visited, and she began to notice that it seemed like everyone at Cibola was planning to go to college, "no matter what." She soon learned that she could always get Cibola students to enroll in her program; in fact, they would take any slots left vacant by the other schools. Since she would pick up the kids at their homes, she began to enjoy getting to know the kids and their parents, and the idea of getting back to working at a high school began to look attractive to her.

It was even more attractive after she became the recruitment and retention officer in Yuma for Northern Arizona University (NAU). In that capacity, she made regular visits to Cibola and found that it was very comforting to be at the school. A year later, in 1995, then-principal Johnny Rico hired García for the freshman counselor position at Cibola, specifically to work with the newly developed freshman teams.

Ms. Becky, as the students often call her, believes she has grown and developed in her counseling position. Being in charge of scholarships, both by finding local contributors and helping students win the scholarships, García became the spokesperson for the school. It didn't take long for Tony Steen to recognize her talents and her strong work ethic, so when the vacancy came up he asked García to become the head of guidance. She was not sure she was ready, but Steen took the time to convince her—and that is where Becky García has been since 2001.

"It's been a lot of hard work," she says, "but yet I think that the philosophy of the Cibola guidance office has never died. It's always been the same." I ask her what she means by that, and she responds, "We're one for all and all for one. We don't work as individual persons; we work as a team." However, she still has trouble asking anyone to do something she hasn't done already because she feels "leaders have to be servants before they can truly be leaders." This echoes Greenleaf's concept of the servant-leader, discussed in Chapter 3.

Continuity Amidst Change

Cibola's guidance office has seen many changes through the years, but it has never lost its way. Successive heads of the department and changes in personnel notwithstanding, the policies and traditions established by Jon Walk and Jim Sullivan have continued. As in any group of strong people who work closely together, there have been conflicts at times. Becky remembers when "Sully had just stepped down as department chair but it was hard for him to let go," and neither he nor Luján liked the freshman teams at the beginning. But Becky just waited them out, and eventually, as she expected, they came around and became great fans of the teams.

As usual, students' needs trumped everything else, and the emphasis on postsecondary education continued to be the counselors' major goal. That remains true in spite of retirements (Sully and Geralyn) and major personnel changes due to the opening of two new schools in the last 4 years. The persistence of the guidance department's mission is a testament to the power of the cause that binds them all.

The Teacher's Role in Counseling

In comparing Cibola to his former school, one teacher says,

[T]he two schools are very different. [The other school] was much larger and [it] is very spread out so there was no sense of community. It was like you were out there by yourself . . . but the physical plant of (Cibola) kind of directs everything inside. . . . [I]n the morning you get the mail, you go through the guidance office and see those guidance counselors and, in my humble opinion, that is why Cibola is different. . . . If I have a problem with a student, as I go through the office I'll stop and say, "Hey, you know, so and so is having a problem." . . . I get feedback: "You're the second teacher to tell me that this week." The guidance staff, I think, is more important than people give them credit for. They . . . coordinate the effort for the student.

This is just one of the ways in which Cibola's teachers interact with the guidance office, but teachers are also important contributors to the counseling and guidance process itself.

IT TAKES A WHOLE SCHOOL

Jim Sullivan understood that in order to carry out his ambitious plan he needed the help of his colleagues. Fortunately, he had a golden opportunity at the very first retreat when Jon Walk brought his leadership team together: The two assistant principals and all the department chairs, including the head of guidance and the manager of grounds, all went to Phoenix for 3 days to write Cibola's mission statement and develop their organizational plan. It was their first opportunity to get to know one another and to sit down and talk without interruptions about Cibola and how they were going to make their dreams a reality.

The retreat provided Sullivan an opportunity to explain his plan for counseling and guidance to the department heads and win their support. He wanted to involve all the teachers in the counseling and guidance process. He believed that the teachers knew their students best and could help them make decisions about what courses to take, so it was important that they participate in the registration process. Sullivan won the department heads over and they, in turn, won over their teachers. They all agreed to be important participants in the guidance process.

The contributions that teachers make, as well as the pride they take in participating, are reflected in one teacher's response to my question: What happens to students who fail, say, biology as freshmen?

> They have one of two choices depending on the teacher—and this is something that is very important, the teacher's recommendation. Does a kid fail because they (*sic*) were lazy, because they didn't put in the effort, which is 90% of the kids who fail? [In this case, the teacher] may put them up for earth science the next year and then tell them they still have to make up the credit in biology later on, so they don't get hit with the same course [that bored them] 2 years in a row. So, a lot of those kids we just move up. Now, they still have to come back to get that biology credit, but giving them a break for a year, I think, is beneficial. . . . Then, in the junior year they can come back and take biology. The nice thing about what we do is that if they really excel—so many of these kids are just clueless as freshmen and sophomores, and, finally, at the time they're near the end of the sophomore year they realize they want to do something—if they're really doing well, we can even put them into chemistry and have them go back and pick up their biology [credit]. But it isn't one of those things where we keep them in the same class time after time . . . because they get very bored. Again, these are the kids who didn't pass because [of] laziness . . . or attendance. Now the kid who doesn't get it but is still interested in biology, the teacher will talk to them and say, "Hey, you want to take biology all over again? You're just missing these key concepts; get them next year and it might be easier." For those . . . kids, it's easier to take the biology right afterward. . . . I think our teachers do a really good job talking to our kids at registration and trying to get them into the right area.

This teacher's spontaneous, if somewhat rambling, description of the process illustrates both the value of the teachers' involvement and Cibola's insistence on individual solutions for common problems. It is not about what it's supposed to be, but about what is best for a particular student.

The connection between teachers and counselors does not end there. Early on, Sully and the rest of the counselors sought the English department's support in the development of several important components of college applications: The résumé, background information, and personal essay. These are tasks that in middle- and upper-class homes are often completed with parental help, and sometimes even with the help of hired consultants. At Cibola, those tasks are a part of the sophomore English curriculum. At this point all Cibola students begin to see themselves as college applicants.

THE SCHOLARSHIP COUNSELOR

Once they had succeeded in opening all their students to the possibilities of further education, the counseling staff had to face the dismal economic reality faced by most of their students' families. As noted earlier, one of the roles of the counselors was to convince parents of the possibilities available to their children when the parents don't have college experience. But the realization of those possibilities involved expenses beyond the parents' reach. So the search for scholarships had to be intensive. But once you open students and parents to larger possibilities you have to deliver, so, as counselor Luján explains:

> I tell the Spanish-speaking parents that they'd better save their money. "*Porque va a costar mucho dinero*" (it's going to cost a lot of money), but "*hay mucha ayuda*" (but there's plenty of help), and the way to get there is to get good grades. . . . There are four people that are involved, highly involved, in making a success of every student that we have: The parent, the student, the teacher, and the counselor. We are a *team*, and we do all our work with the students as a team. You keep track of your kid at home, you tell me what's going on there, because I have 400 or so kids that I've got to take care of.

From the beginning, Sully and the other counselors, Helen Rice in particular, went into classes to talk about how students should apply for scholarships and to give them inside information, such as urging them to pay special attention to those applications that required essays and speeches because the competition was thinner for those scholarships. The counselors encouraged the students to spend time after school in the counseling office, where all application materials are carefully filed within students' reach, and go over the scholarship and summer programs to find out what the requirements were so they would be ready to apply by their senior year.

Sometime between their junior and senior years, students develop a résumé and a life story upon which teachers can base reference letters to include in their portfolios. This recurring process communicates the school community's high aspirations for their students and also keeps students' attention focused on their plans for the future.

According to Toni Badone, from the very beginning Cibola's counselors strongly emphasized starting the senior packet preparation early. Its components—the résumé and the personal essay—were explained to the students during their freshman year. The idea was for students to become aware of the importance of earning good grades and gathering experiences to enrich the final product—that is, their senior packet. The students are able to update their senior packet during credit check time every year and, therefore, to view their progress. By the beginning of their senior year, the students have accumulated the material and skills to fine-tune their personal essays with ease.

Early on, the weight and intensity of all these responsibilities became overwhelming to the counselors and led to the creation of a new position: scholarship counselor, a full-time person devoted to the search for scholarships and the application process to follow. They did this by turning a faculty position into a counseling position. The first scholarship counselor in a Yuma high school was hired by Cibola in 1990, just in time for Cibola's first graduating class in 1991. The person in that position took over the many ancillary pre-graduation tasks that the counselors had been providing since the school's opening.

The encouragement handed out by all the adults at Cibola—be they teacher, custodian, police officer, cafeteria attendant, or principal—results in a rush of applications for admissions and scholarships to universities and community colleges in the spring of every year. Cibola's counselors are rightly proud of the large number of applications sent out by their students every year and the amount of resources that they represent. Recruiters who visit the school have recognized and commented on their extraordinary effort.

As head of guidance, Becky García has adopted Sully's determination to guide students into a future beyond high school. That was, and continues to be, the goal shared by all the counselors at the school. Their relentless efforts have led to amazing successes for a school with the kind of demographics that others cite to excuse failure.

By 2009, across 19 graduations, 31 Cibola graduates had been accepted into U.S. military academies. All but one of them completed the program. Another 9 Cibola graduates (half of them Latino[a]s) have been selected as Flinn Scholars through the annual competition funded by the Flinn Foundation of Arizona with the purpose of retaining the "best and brightest" in the state. Cibola has also recognized 17 National Merit Finalists as well as several AP scholars and one AP Honors scholar. And in the school's 20-year history, 14 Cibola High School athletic teams have been awarded the Arizona Interscholastic Association's highest award, the Scholar Athlete Team Award. In the aggregate, all those scholarships amount to millions of dollars every year, sometimes as much as 10 million.

Those achievements are the reward for the many hours that Cibola's counselors and faculty spend at their jobs. Theirs are not 9-to-3 positions. The counselors are at school early and leave late, and sometimes various evening activities may also call them back to the school. There are, for example, military and Flinn Nights when parents and students are invited to attend to learn what is involved in obtaining scholarships through those sources. There are also continuous phone calls to secure even more opportunities for their students.

Conrad Luján, for example, is the point person for the military academies. He spends hours on the phone getting information from the legislative offices responsible for recommending students for the available openings so he may properly advice interested students. He has done this for so long and so well that, as I found out, he is known far beyond Cibola.

I called the office of one of Arizona's senators to ask for information regarding the schools that send applications for the military academies. The person to whom I spoke responded that most applications came from the so-called "academic" schools. She named a few to illustrate that many of them were private or "prep" schools. I asked whether any of the public schools applied at all, and she responded: "Well, there's one school, Cibola, in Yuma, that always sends 6 or 7 applications. The counselor there always makes sure that students complete everything and checks on them." That is, of course, what it takes to ensure that Cibola's students' applications stand out against the stiff competition.

Cibola's counselors actively seek out students to apply for scholarships, especially those given by local organizations. Becky García recalls attending a scholarship presentation banquet where 10 of the 11 scholarships were awarded to Cibola students. After the ceremony, representatives of the organization commented that Cibola's "packaging" of their students far surpassed the other schools', and that they could have easily given all 11 of the scholarships to Cibola students.

Packaging a student is a time-consuming task. Becky recalls a year when she had four applicants for a major scholarship:

> It took me 2 months to package those kids. Every weekend, I'd come and work for 1 hour . . . because I want to make sure that I'm doing the best job I possibly can for a particular kid. . . . What leaves Cibola has to be crystal clean; that's just our philosophy.

This is another example of the "Cibola Way" at work.

In addition to all the work that counseling and guidance entail, there's the personal investment I have seen counselors make on behalf of students who desperately need them—in some cases going far beyond what their positions call for, as Becky did in the case of Nina that follows.

NINA'S GRADUATION

Although Cibola's goal is to send all their students on to further education—be it college, trade, or the military—for a few students, just completing high school is an almost unachievable goal. Cibola's counselors do the best they can for those students by making sure that they receive, at the very least, their high school diploma. Nina was one of those students.

It was the end of the semester and time to close the books. Graduation day was approaching. Nina, a 20-year-old young woman, had been working hard to complete her credits so she could receive her diploma. Becky had worked with Nina and her mother to ensure that the girl would earn her diploma before she turned 21 (at which time she would no longer be eligible to attend Arizona public schools). At that point, her only options would be taking the GED or enrolling, and paying for, community college courses—all of which would strain both her budget and her time.

García had taken a special interest in this girl because Nina had almost left school after she became pregnant. Her mother had advised her to drop out so she could get a job. Becky spoke at length with Nina's mother, explaining to her how difficult it would be for Nina to get a decent job without a high school diploma. Once Nina's mother was convinced, Ms. Becky helped Nina plan a way to complete all her missing credits by using the resources available for high school students in Yuma (to be discussed in Chapter 5). Nina followed her advice and, according to her counselor's final check, it seemed she would be able to graduate.

That is, until the afternoon of graduation day, when the registrar found a mistake: Nina was missing one credit. Becky couldn't believe it, but the registrar appeared to be correct. She went looking for the assistant principal for academics and called Nina's math teacher, whose class it was. In the meantime, Nina was informed of the error. She was crushed; she had been waiting to get the okay to call her mother and tell her the good news, and now that wasn't going to happen.

Nina was outside with her husband crying while the assistant principal for academics, Becky, and the math teacher tried to untangle the problem. The teacher finally cleared the error. It wasn't Becky's fault; Nina had indeed completed all her credits. All the administrators were informed and Becky went to look for Nina. The happy ending was celebrated with hugs, and even some tears. Nina was one among the few Cibola graduates who have had to, at least for the moment, be content with only a high school diploma.

Jon Walk's determination to create a school where all students could succeed and Jim Sullivan's similar enthusiasm for his job and passion for student success have served the school well. So has the total commitment of the staff, as Becky García explains: "Our students are normal students you would find on any high school campus, but the people who work with them in the classroom, on the athletic field, and the support staff all believe in them." She believes that the main reason Cibola has been successful is the commitment of the faculty, staff, students, and their parents to making Cibola a family community:

> At least half of Cibola's incoming freshmen, from the day Cibola High School opened its doors, arrive at less than a 6th-grade level in reading or math. The collaboration between the different departments in order to ensure a positive learning environment for our students is what has made the difference. . . . Passion and commitment are huge components of the Cibola mystique. The passion to work with our students at the academic levels they come with, and then witnessing their growth, has enabled us to have successful students.

Chapter Five

English for
English Learners

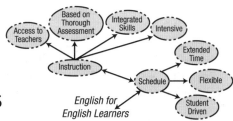

Perhaps the greatest challenge that Walk and Sullivan faced in their quest to get all their Cibola students not just through high school but beyond was the demographics of the student population they would be welcoming to the school. I have noted this briefly in earlier chapters, but let us now take another look back at Yuma County as described in the 1990 census. That will give us a better understanding of the population the Cibola staff faced when the school opened in 1988. The data were drawn from the county census because Yuma City was not yet large enough to be analyzed as a separate entity.

DEMOGRAPHIC BACKGROUND

By 1990, Yuma County's population had reached almost 100,000, and just below 20% of that population was foreign-born—almost double the state average of 12.5%. Given that fact, it is not surprising that many of Yuma County's residents—over a third of the county's total population—reported speaking "a language other than English," compared to just under a fifth statewide. The 1990 census reported an average per household income of $35,827 for Yuma County, but 6,369 of those households reported yearly incomes of less than $10,000.

Educationally speaking, among the 63,000 of those who were 25 years old and over in Yuma County during the 1990 census, 20% reported less than a ninth-grade education, only a little more than 20% had graduated from high school (compared to the state's 83.5% graduation rate), and less than 20% had achieved degrees in higher education (compared to 27% statewide). Thus, as a group, the students who entered Cibola were poorer than the state's population, from families with less years of schooling, and were more likely to speak English as a second language.[1]

THE MIGRANT POPULATION

The population also varied in response to the migrant stream. Families following the harvest arrived and departed in response to the needs of the farmers. Unfortunately, school calendars were incompatible with the harvest. According to Anne Stadler, who worked in the Yuma area for many years, the families would arrive in Yuma around October or November but the high schools would not accept the students until January. That was the case until a civil rights suit in the late 1970s required the high schools to admit the migrant students upon arrival.[2]

However, admission to the high schools did not ensure good instruction. There were no trained teachers or formal programs for the English language learners (ELLs). Additional civil rights suits followed, and by the mid-1980s Stadler was able to hire trainers for the teachers, not just at the high schools but also at the feeder schools. Summer programs were instituted for the students and a set of books was created that the migrant students could take with them wherever they went. Those portable books allowed them to complete five basic courses on their own time. By 1990, the Yuma Union High School District had bought all of the coursework, and the self-study books became available to anyone in the district who was behind in credits. Also by that time, Stadler was able to get Arizona Western College (AWC) and Northern Arizona University (NAU) involved in preparing teachers for the increasing population of English learners.

CIBOLA'S CHALLENGE

All of this preceded the opening of Cibola in 1988. The Walk-Sullivan team and the rest of the staff were not ignorant of the educational needs of many of their incoming students. In fact, Walk and Sullivan had both been peripherally involved with Stadler's activities. As vice principal at Kofa (one of the other two high schools in Yuma), Walk had come face-to-face with the difficulties involved in providing a proper education to migrant students, and Sullivan had been a frequent speaker at parent meetings held by Stadler.

Both Walk and Sullivan were already well aware that language was going to pose a large barrier to their stated intentions in their new school. Everyone knew that a high level of competence in the English language was an essential asset for success in high school. But Cibola was promising more than that: They were emphasizing education beyond high school. How were they to fulfill the promises they were making to their entering students?

Walk did not know much about the teaching of ELLs, and although Sullivan had been both a language teacher and a language learner, he was not familiar with the instructional strategies that would make it possible for poor adolescents to become skilled in English while simultaneously absorbing, in their new language, the academic content necessary for advancing on to higher education. That was the challenge that the Cibola staff was facing: In just 4 years, they aimed to provide the many students who would enter the school with, at best, a rudimentary knowledge of English with the linguistic and academic knowledge necessary to continue on to college.

Many other schools were facing a similar challenge in the 1980s. As the Latino(a) population was growing throughout the country, the numbers of English language learners increased by 105%, but their growth was not matched with a corresponding growth in ELL teachers.[3] That was a challenge to educators everywhere, but it is probably fair to say that, other than Cibola, no high school with a primarily Latino(a) population was promising all its entering students, including English learners, a path to college.

The dramatic increase in ELLs came at a time when there was a dearth of scholarly guidance for the instruction of ELLs at the secondary level. Although there was already a (mostly ignored) body of research regarding instruction for English language learners in the early years of school, that was not, and is still not, true for the secondary level. In fact, Faltis and Wolfe determined that "there was virtually no research on secondary level ESL instruction before 1990."[4] Even by 2004, when the Northwest Regional Educational Laboratory decided to conduct a review of the literature on ELLs at the high school level, the pickings were few. They began with 200 studies, but that number was reduced to 73, and then eventually further pared down to only 20 studies of the rigor and value they were seeking. So, back in 1988, there was very little help available for Cibola, even beyond Yuma or Arizona. Given the scant knowledge in that area, the problem was not an easy one to solve.

SOLVING THE PROBLEM

Fortunately for Cibola's future, Walk had become acquainted with Bob Brekke at his former school. At that time, Bob Brekke was perhaps the only teacher in Yuma with the determination necessary to teach English learners. He was eager for the challenges represented by the new school and ready to leave an environment where he felt the Latino(a) students were dismissed as unable to accomplish much.

"Walk was a revolutionary," says Brekke, so he applied to move to Cibola with him. Brekke thinks he was chosen because "I was hard-working, open to new ideas, and active in change." He adds, "If it had not been for Jon Walk, I would have left Yuma." Not only did Brekke stay in Yuma, but through a federal grant, he was also able to complete his MS in ESL instruction.

Brekke taught all three Structured English Immersion (SEI) classes when Cibola opened and remembers that it was a long struggle to get more SEI hours because they didn't have the teacher allocations. Jon Walk was able to keep the SEI class small for a while, but as the population increased, so did the class size.

Growth

Increases in the numbers of ELL students was what brought Irma Preciado to the SEI classroom. Irma, who until recently headed the ELL department at Cibola, was young and inexperienced when Principal Jon Walk plucked her out of a permanent substitute teacher role. He needed an additional teacher for English learners in order to split up a large class. Irma was bilingual, and Walk was impressed by her effectiveness in teaching a large, all-boy tech class, so he asked her to take the ESL job. When she confessed her ignorance about ESL to him, he set her up with Bob Brekke, who became her mentor. It did not take Preciado long to gain confidence and begin taking some of the newly available classes on ESL instruction at Northern Arizona University. She soon completed her master's degree in that area and eventually became the head of the ESL department at Cibola.

Irma recalls her first time teaching ESL at Cibola: "I had Native Americans in the classroom [and] I had special education students in the classroom, together with kids who had just arrived from Mexico." Through her courses, Brekke's mentorship, and her own classroom experience, Irma began to realize that what they were doing was not right. There was no ESL department at that time, but with everyone's support Preciado and Brekke were able to initiate changes while still under the English department.

A few years later, Brekke was named head of the English department, and, with his knowledge and experience, he began to do what was needed to more directly improve ESL instruction. It was not long before ESL became a separate department under Brekke's leadership. Irma Preciado says, "He has a lot of knowledge about ESL and what it entails and what needs to be done. So we pretty much still use all his ideas." That continuity was facilitated when Preciado followed Brekke as head of ESL.

Bob Brekke and Irma Preciado became the architects of the present program for students who enter Cibola with low levels of skills in the English language. The program is well-grounded on the latest recommendations of researchers in that area. It is also designed to ensure that English learners are able to compete well for the post–high school opportunities that the guidance office secures each year for Cibola's graduates.

Induction into SEI

The induction of an English learner into the Cibola structure begins with conversations between Cibola's teachers and teachers from the sending schools. The latter help identify those students who may not be able to participate effectively in the standard academic program without additional intensive instruction in English. Those students are tested by a specialist who makes a placement recommendation to the ESL teachers, who then take it from there. Bob Brekke explains:

> [T]hey're placed in Level I, II, III, or IV. They get 3 years at Level I or II, and a year ago we started 2 years at Level III instead of only 1 year because we found out it just wasn't enough time. And that's helped a lot; in fact, at [the beginning of the] semester we moved eight students out into regular English. I think a big part of that is that extra hour of instruction each day at Level III. And at Level IV we still have just 1 hour. I would like to have 2 hours with them, too, because if we're supposed to get them up to native speakers' ability in reading and writing, there's just so much to do.

As is evident in this ELL teacher's comments, flexibility is an essential component of Cibola's ESL sequence: "At [the beginning of the] semester we moved eight students out into regular English"—that is, the decision was made jointly by the teachers in the ESL program and those receiving them into the regular English program. The students were not trapped within an established schedule. There was no point in keeping them in a class that they had outgrown, so they were moved on to face bigger challenges. The students also benefited from a schedule change made by the teachers: the addition of an extra hour to Level III—a change made not for bureaucratic reasons, but in response to the faculty's collective assessment of what might benefit their students. That small change made a big difference to those eight students. Finally, notice that the ESL program's goal is to get the students up "to native speakers' ability in reading and writing"—high expectations indeed.

Rigor

The sense of urgency required by those expectations is apparent in Bob Brekke's voice as he explains what that means to him: "I learned that an entering student at a top university would know 130,000 words and compared that to the ELL freshman at Cibola, who may know 100 words in English. Well, to get them from 100 to 130,000, in 3 or 4 years [is] a big job." I ask if it can be done, and he responds with a careful computation of the task at hand:

> If we only expect them to get to 60,000 and we have 180 days times 4 [years]. If you do the math, 100 [words]/day isn't going to get them to 60,000, never mind 130,000. . . . [Y]ou can probably survive in a community college with a 60,000-word vocabulary. But you can't do it in 10 words per week or even 20 per week. You have to do 100 per day at least. Well, the only way you do that is through reading. . . . One hour every day. That's their only homework. Seven days a week.

Bob uses a program consisting of library books labeled according to difficulty, each accompanied by a test. Students choose the books they want to read and earn points according to the book's difficulty and their scores on the tests. He adds: "I'm proud to say that my EL kids are outscoring the regular English kids on the points earned for Accelerated Readers. . . . Last year, at the end of the year, we had doubled what the freshman kids were doing in points earned."

The reading program is complemented by the journal that each student is required to keep. The journal takes the place of the traditional book report. It is where students react to their daily recreational reading. The teacher provides a set of questions that "encourage [students] to make . . . predictions. . . . [I]t keeps them interested in the book and . . . makes them look outside of the reading and bring in their own life experiences . . . to have them apply higher-level thinking." Journals are checked every Friday to ensure both the quantity (one entry for each day) and the quality of writing. As a result, students in Brekke's Level III class end up reading about 50 books per school year. Bob puts it in stark terms:

> If you were to tell a kid at the beginning of the year, "Okay, you're going to read a 1,000-page book and do a 100-page report on it," they'd be down at the counselor's office. . . . And when you can get ESL kids to write 100 pages minimum, but most of them will write 100–150 pages in response to what they've read . . . that's just a tremendous amount of writing that's all done on their own, after school, on the weekends.

Flexibility

I was introduced to the demanding yet flexible Cibola ESL program several years ago when I learned about Guadalupe's case. Guadalupe was one of six students in one of the focus groups I interviewed during my initial explorations at Cibola High School. She had just arrived from Mexico and had started that year at Cibola as a sophomore although she spoke no English. She was able to participate fully because, although she spoke only Spanish, the other five students in that group were bilingual. When we spoke about personal goals, Guadalupe said she loved math and was thinking that she might be a math teacher. I encouraged her, pointing out that bilingual skills would make it easier to get a teaching job.

A year later, I saw Guadalupe in Brekke's class while observing there. I asked him about her progress, and he told me that she was a hard worker. In fact, they had put her in honors English after she completed her year in Level II. She didn't seem to be doing well, so they decided to bring her back to Level II. However, Guadalupe refused to leave the honors class. Instead, in tears, she promised her teachers that she would work really hard. She stayed in honors English, and then honors history was also added to her program. The teacher in the latter class did not realize that Guadalupe was an ESL student because she had earned more points than anyone else in the class.

In Brekke's class, Guadalupe also read the most books and filled out the most journals in response to her reading. She went on to get three associate's degrees (in math, physics, and engineering) at Arizona Western College, and she then moved to Arizona State University, where she received her BS in electrical engineering in May 2008. She is now employed at a large corporation in Arizona.

Carlos González, a former ESL student at Cibola, recalls his arrival at the school in 1993. He was totally monolingual. The next 4 years went as follows: He had three 1-hour classes of English plus sheltered classes in world history, typing, and physical education. He progressed so well that he was moved on to ESL II. By his second year, Carlos was moved out of sheltered classes and into the regular program and eventually moved on to regular English and all the classes required for graduation in his senior year. He went on to Arizona Western College, where he was awarded a soccer scholarship. Two and a half years later, Carlos received his Associate degree in general studies. That was followed by work as substitute or assistant teacher until he was able to fulfill his dream of completing his BA and returning to Cibola as a teacher in the ESL department working alongside his former teachers.

The sheltered classes that Carlos took are Cibola's answer to the unavoidable gap between non–English speakers and the academic program necessary for college admission. Those classes allow students to move on with some assistance until they are ready to compete in the regular classes. Sheltered classes and ESL are complemented by electives such as choir or theatre, which are language-rich but not as cognitively demanding. The sequence is not prescribed; it is adjusted to the needs and progress of each student.

The flexibility in Cibola's ESL program is a quality that is missing in most of the ESL programs I have observed. It is also an aspect missing from the scant research available on ESL at the secondary level. The lack of flexibility can be a real problem for students who are likely to enter such programs at various degrees of competence in English, as well as varied immigrant status, as documented by Norrid-Lacey.[5]

Norrid-Lacey's study of Hispanic high school students is one of the few studies of that population conducted at the secondary level. In the high school she studied, ESL students could choose just one of two tracks: mainstream or ESL. Just two tracks. Students feared the mainstream track because of conflicts with the English-speaking students, but long-term placement in the ESL track led to English learners' linguistic and social segregation, thereby limiting their ability to become fluent English speakers. The consequences for the students were grave. At the end of 4 years, only 27% of the ESL freshman cohort in the study received their diplomas.

This situation should not be seen as an aberration. There are many schools running similar programs in the country. But the even larger problem may be that the Latino(a) dropout problem appears to be, in part, a function of English learners not being served by either English as a Second Language (ESL) or bilingual programs. It is also important to note that, unlike many other schools with similar populations, Cibola implicitly recognizes the value of the students' home language. Spanish for native speakers and honors and AP Spanish are offered at Cibola. The advantage native speakers can enjoy in those classes provides a balance against the inherent disadvantage they experience while studying a standard curriculum designed for English learners.

Chapter Six

Continued Improvement and Alternate Paths to Success

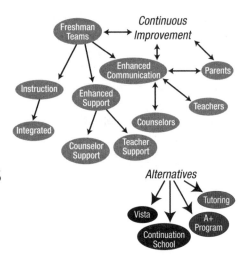

Through over 20 years of operation serving more than 40,000 students, the aggregation of students, staff, and administrators called Cibola has not stood still. Like Collins and Porras's "visionary companies," Cibola has continued to evolve as it responds to the challenges that arise while retaining the core values, operating strategies, and cultural practices that have distinguished it from the beginning.[1]

In the following pages, we will discuss some of the practices that made Cibola different from the start as well as those that have been adopted in response to perceived problems. Throughout the school's history, all changes have been driven by the devotion to the school's major responsibility: To ensure that all students have the opportunity to learn what they need to learn in order to reach their goals. That is the common thread that runs through this chapter.

THE IMPORTANCE OF TIME

The deliberate emphasis on time as an important resource for instruction was noted by Edmonds in his analysis of effective schools: "Effective schools get that way partly by making it clear that pupil acquisition of basic school skills takes precedence over all other activities."[2] Berliner was able to demonstrate the importance of differentiating allocated time from the academic learning time—that is, the portion of allocated time actually devoted to teaching.[3]

Thus, from the beginning, Cibola's staff sought to maximize instructional time by removing as many distractions as possible. One of the first things noticed by teachers as they arrive at their new classrooms is that there are no clocks on the wall. Jon Walk believed that clocks presented and unnecessary distraction to instruction so, to this day, there are no clocks in Cibola's classrooms. The PA system, or "intercom," one of the most commonly disliked source of interruptions to instruction, was reduced to once-daily morning announcements at Cibola, and the 35-minute rule, imposed somewhat later, allows teachers a block of uninterrupted instructional time immediately after the second bell rings. Most recently, under Tony Steen's leadership the "tardy sweep" was adopted to protect instructional time while also removing an unnecessary burden from teachers. The "sweep" allows teachers to get started with class right away without having to interrupt class to discipline students coming in late.

The Tardy Sweep

This is how the tardy sweep works: Students have 6 minutes to get from one class to the next. At the 5-minute mark, a warning bell rings to remind students that they have only 1 more minute before the tardy bell sounds. All along the way, teachers (on their planning period) or administrators will direct students to keep moving along. The staff knows there may be special circumstances that can be worked out with a student and that some may need help to solve a potential problem, but, in general, students who are not in their classrooms when the tardy bell sounds are sent to the "tardy sweep" room. They are not counted absent, but they are responsible for any work they miss in class.

In the tardy sweep room, one of the campus security guards records the tardies on a spreadsheet that indicates how many tardies the student has accrued. The security guard also calls the parents at home or work to let them know their child was late and asks for their help in getting their child to class on time. The tardiness is recorded and indicated on the student's attendance record. More than six tardies will result in a half-day's suspension but that does not happen often, and, according to Steen, is more likely an indicator of more serious problems that need to be addressed.

Being in the tardy sweep room is not fun. Students sit on a chair, not at a desk; they are not allowed to speak, sleep, do homework, study for tests, or engage in any other distractions. They can work on materials to prepare them for the state or college admission tests if they wish. Other than that, the tardy sweep room is very boring; it's just a place to keep students from interrupting instruction in their classrooms and, hopefully, to discourage them from being tardy in the future.

After-School

At Cibola, instructional time is also extended beyond the school day and school year through summer school, before- and afterschool programs, and various forms of personal and computer-based tutoring. All of those measures serve as a daily reminder that instruction is the most important purpose of the school.[4] In spite of this continued emphasis, some students need even more time to learn and to focus on their studies, so the Cibola staff developed additional ways to extend instruction.

FULFILLING THE MISSION

Cibola High School began as, and continues to be, a school driven by a mission of excellence for everyone, from the administrators to the students. Since the school's inception, excellence for students has been defined by the pursuit of a life plan beyond high school. This lofty ideal was, and is, particularly ambitious given the demographics of the school's student population. Cibola's achievements have been predicated on the staff's willingness to see every problem as a challenge to be solved. Solutions may be borrowed from other schools, from research, and from common sense. The constant focus behind every one of the strategies or initiatives that has been adopted has been: Will this help our students achieve their goals?

The value of this approach to the school's goals is made visible in the school careers of Cibola's students. Several of those I have followed have benefited from programs that encouraged them to stay in school (see Natriello, Pallas, & Alexander, 1989). Through the availability of alternative settings and strategies such as the Vista Alternative School, the Continuation School, the A+ program (a computer-driven way for students to make up missed work), and the "packets" that allow those who are behind in their credits to make them up in time for graduation, Cibola entices even the most recalcitrant students to complete their work, to graduate, and to continue on with further education.

Most of the alternatives and innovations discussed below began within the bubbling cauldron of Cibola's early years, and many have migrated beyond Cibola to all the schools within the Yuma Union High School District. The history of that evolution, from school to school to district, will be discussed in the concluding chapter of the book.

VISTA ALTERNATIVE SCHOOL

The ideas that led to Vista Alternative School, for example, arose very early out of concerns that Walk and his administrative team had about those students who, in spite of their efforts, were clearly on the road to dropping out. The department chairs knew who they were: students who missed classes and, when they came, did not even try to complete their work, thus failing to accumulate any credits during their freshman year. Something had to be done to ensure that they stayed in school through graduation, so the Cibola faculty came up with the STAR program.

Toni Badone, then chair of the English department, remembers how they created the STAR program as an alternative for students who were not succeeding in the regular program: "It was a school-within-a-school aimed at students who were not progressing and could fall through the cracks"—second-year students with no earned credits, for example. The success of Cibola's STAR program motivated the superintendent to consider opening a similar districtwide alternative for all of Yuma's high school students: "If this works in your campus [Cibola], we'll look for funding to do it in the district for everybody." And that was how the Vista Alternative School came to be. For the first couple of years, Cibola's students predominated at the new alternative school, but it was not long before the other high schools began to suggest the Vista Alternative to their students.

Today, counselors all over the Yuma Union High School District refer students to Vista, where they find the many alternative avenues that have evolved in response to their needs. The students like what Vista has to offer: Smaller classes, self-paced independent study, a more flexible schedule, and, perhaps most important for some students, few distractions.

Students can complete all their credits at Vista or return to their home schools when they are ready—an unlikely choice, according to former principal Chris Magdaleno: "After they're here [at Vista], 99% of them do not want to go back to their home school. They like the setting here, they like the small classes, and they like the atmosphere at the school." In either case, once they complete the 22 credits required for graduation, Vista students can choose to walk the graduation line with their friends back at their home schools.

Not all students can meet Vista's standards, explains Magdaleno: "What we don't take here," he says, "are some of the kids who are discipline problems; a lot of insubordination, a lot of defiance of authority, those are the type of kids that do not fit here." Those students are sent back to their home schools but can reapply if they go through a semester without another referral.

Attendance and good grades are the hallmarks of success at Vista, in addition to good behavior: "We have very few behavior problems here," says Magdaleno, "because the kids come over here with the understanding that we're doing them a favor by letting them come here. . . . Vista has a waiting list." Small 2-hour classes of no more than 20 students are one of the key ingredients in Vista's success. Students go to two classes a day, and every 6 weeks they receive their half-credit in the chosen class. This strategy fits well with students who need frequent feedback to remain engaged in learning.

There's even more to Vista, as I learned from Ramona Crumby, who is in charge of dropout prevention at the school. She introduced me to the Learning Lab (LL), a program developed by a former Vista principal. Ramona, in turn, created the "learning packets," each of which covers content equivalent to what a class in a regular school would cover in a semester. The packets are organized by chapters, each one followed by a test that the students take at the LL.

Working with the packets at Vista starts with the home school counselor, who fills out the necessary forms specifying what instruction the student needs to recapture the credits they have lost. Crumby explains, "If a student is having difficulty with a packet . . . all they have to do is sign in for an appointment with one of the teachers." The teacher at the LL also fills out the report card, which is sent back to the student's home school at the completion of each packet. "They can receive as many credits as we have available as long as they go through their home schools." Decisions about graduation are also made at the students' home schools, where their Vista transcripts will be evaluated to determine whether they have met all the criteria for graduation.

Vista continues to evolve and grow. Most recently, under the direction of Principal Molly Kelly, the school has attained North Central accreditation and that is likely to lead to some changes. With its 96% attendance rate and 75% graduation rate in 2007, Vista is becoming a real player among its big sisters in the Yuma Union High School District.

VISTA'S CONTRIBUTION TO STUDENT SUCCESS

Three of the students in my sample, each for different reasons, graduated after completing their respective high school programs through Vista. Sarita, an above-average student and ebullient young woman, wanted to be a doctor one day and a beautician the next, but she got pregnant at age 16. She enrolled in Vista immediately and graduated with her class in 2008. Braulia had difficulty with her schoolwork from the beginning, but she was persistent. She attended summer school at the end of both her freshman and sophomore years, but she was still missing many credits in her junior year. She transferred to Vista and graduated in 2009. Ana was a solid B student at the end of her first semester at Cibola, but by the end of her second semester, her grades began to slide. She was down to a low C when she decided to transfer to Vista. She completed all the rest of her credits at Vista and graduated with her class in 2008.

All three of these girls might have dropped out if it weren't for the Vista alternative, but all of them were able to finish. None of those students had behavior or discipline problems. Those who do and are therefore excluded from Vista may attend the Continuation School, the alternative available for YUHSD students who get into big trouble.

THE CONTINUATION SCHOOL

The Continuation School operates under Vista, but it works directly through the schools. It is designed to provide a way for students on long-term suspension (i.e., suspended for a full semester) to continue their education while they are forbidden to attend any other high school in the district. Students and parents must agree to the provisions of an enrollment, attendance, and discipline contract that stipulates the behaviors required to remain enrolled in the program, including strict adherence to the assigned schedule.

The Continuation School offers students like Ángel, a high-achieving student in my sample who made a big mistake, a way to keep up with their classes while on long-term suspension. Ángel was given a 6-month suspension when he got involved in a situation where beer was brought to a school function. He attended the Continuation School and completed all the credits he needed during the fall semester of his senior year. He returned to Cibola in the spring, finished his program, and graduated in the top quarter of his class.

Although the students at the Continuation School are there as a consequence of major infractions, the place resembles a busy office, with every student sitting at a computer. Unlike Vista, where you may see artwork on the walls and movement along the halls or in the Learning Lab, the Continuation School appears unidirectional. All eyes are on the computers, and there are no distractions on the walls or in the surrounding area. The only sound you hear is the clicking of the keys. This kind of environment ensures that distractible students can concentrate on their work.

Perhaps the most interesting characteristic of Vista and the Continuation School is the schools' apparent neutrality toward the students. Neither school is designed to warehouse potential dropouts. Instead, both offer students a different learning environment where they can proceed toward their goals, at their own pace, in a calmer, more adult atmosphere than the typical high school.

There is no shame regarding attendance at Vista because the students there are not just "losers." Because the Learning Center is housed in the same area, some of Vista's students are there because they want to get ahead in their credits. According to former principal Magdaleno:

> Vista is more or less a credit retrieval program. The original philosophy was for the students to come over here, get caught up in their credits, and then . . . go back to their home schools. Well, after they're here, 99% of them do not want to go back to their home school. They like the setting here, they like the small classes, and they like the atmosphere at the school so they decide. If they want to stay . . . they can stay here.

That was the decision made by the three young women described earlier. Vista was their choice. All of them could have returned to Cibola, but they chose to stay at Vista because it provided them more flexibility and control over their studies and, therefore, their lives.

Vista's diversity of options, its flexibility, and supportive environment makes it a desirable choice for many students. It also responds to advocates of alternative education who have argued that a variety of educational options is essential for schools seeking to meet the needs of all students.[5] It also sets the school apart from the generality of alternative schools across the country described by the NCES in its recently published survey of public alternative schools.[6]

The NCES survey revealed that in about half of the districts offering alternative education programs, a variety of inappropriate behaviors were sufficient reason, in themselves, for transfer out of a regular school: "possession, distribution, or use of alcohol or drugs (52%); physical attacks or fights; chronic truancy; continual academic failure; possession or use of a weapon other than a firearm; disruptive verbal behavior; and possession or use of a firearm."[7] Note that these are all behavior problems, indicating that, unlike Yuma's Vista, a large number of the country's alternative schools are most likely to be addressing behavior problems rather than students who are in need of a different approach or of more individual attention. So, although over 75% of the districts with alternative schools surveyed by the NCES had curricula leading to a high school diploma, these settings, unlike Vista, may discourage students from pursuing that goal.

FRESHMAN AND INTERDISCIPLINARY TEAMS

Now let us move back to discuss the changes within Cibola itself. The freshman teams were latecomers to Cibola, but they have become a trademark of the school and have now been extended to all YUHSD schools. They were initiated gradually and somewhat serendipitously.

Toni Badone, one of the first English teachers at Cibola, worked with Ben, a history teacher, to provide their students with a well-articulated curriculum in cooperative learning environments. Their success was noted by an assistant principal who was familiar with the research regarding interdisciplinary teams at the middle-school level and who wanted to try the idea with freshmen at Cibola.

To facilitate their work, the vice principal arranged the following semester's schedule so that two of Toni Badone's and Ben's classes were offered back-to-back. That allowed them time to plan together and also gave them a two-period block to integrate world history and English. That was the beginning of what was to become Cibola's freshman teams. The strategy was not formalized until a few years later, when Johnny Rico became vice principal of the school.

Cibola's freshman class is divided into four teams for their core academic courses. Students stay with their team throughout their freshman year. This strategy is similar to the Talent Development School Model, which has been successfully adopted by high-poverty, high-minority schools in Maryland.[8] At Cibola, two counselors stay in close touch with their new students throughout the freshman year. The counselors visit their classes twice a week, meet with the students' teachers every week, and, if necessary, provide individual counseling. This sort of monitoring and guidance was found to be an element of successful intervention programs by Gándara and Bial.[9] It is also among the strategies recommended by the Coalition of Campus Schools Project.[10]

Rico believes that Cibola's freshman teams "played a huge role in a lot of the successes we experienced." By the time he was in his third year as principal, the dropout rate had gone down from 7% to about 2.3% or 2.8%, where it currently hovers.

How did that happen? Although Rico thinks freshman teaming was one of the contributors, he believes the other one was getting the counselors to focus on freshmen. He felt that in the past students were falling through the cracks because the counselors were focusing so much on preparing juniors and seniors for graduation that the freshman and sophomore classes were being left behind: "[T]he stats showed that our highest percentage of dropouts were coming out of the sophomore group."

Rico brought in the counseling team and asked them about the possibility of devoting counselors strictly to the freshmen teams. In spite of the counselors' initial concern that the juniors and seniors were going to suffer from that change, they were delighted when they found that working with the freshman teams gave them the opportunity to talk to the younger students almost daily and to give and receive feedback about students' progress, their 4-year plans, and all that would be necessary for them to pursue education beyond high school.

What is most significant in this review of alternatives is the continuous search for improvement that has characterized the school all through its history. Cibola High School has been continually successful due to its trademark policy of looking at problems, searching for a solution, and placing the solutions under scrutiny for further improvement.

References

Achieve (2010). *Closing the expectations gap: Fifth American state project report*. Retrieved March 1, 2010, from www.achieve.org/closingtheexpectationsgapw010

Ancess, J., & Wichterle Ort, S. (1999). *How the coalition of campus schools have reimagined high school: Seven years later*. New York: National Center for Restructuring Schools, Education, and Teaching.

Bandura, A. (1997). *Self-efficacy: The exercise of control*. New York: W. H. Freeman.

Beck, L. G., & Murphy, J. (1993). *Understanding the principalship: Metaphorical themes, 1920s–1990s*. New York: Teachers College Press.

Berliner, D. (1990). What's all the fuss about instructional time? In M. Ben-Peretz & R. Bromme (Eds.), *The nature of time in schools: Theoretical concepts, practitioner perceptions*. New York: Teachers College Press.

Board on Testing and Assessment and the National Research Council. (October 5, 2009). *Letter report to the U.S. department of education on the race to the top fund*. Available online at http://www.nap.edu/catalog.php?record_id=12780. Washington, DC: National Academies Press.

Center for Policy Studies, Education Research and Community Development. (1998). *Open and closed campuses* (research brief). Retrieved January 28, 2010, from http://icee.isu.edu/Policy/RBClosedvsOpen.pdf

Choy, S. (2001). *Students whose parents did not go to college: Postsecondary access, persistence, and attainment* (NCES 2001–126). Washington, DC: U.S. Department of Education, National Center for Education Statistics.

Coleman, J. S. (1966). *Equality of educational opportunity (EEOS) study*. Washington, DC: U.S. Department of Health, Education, and Welfare, Office of Education.

Collins, J., & Porras, J. I. (1994). *Built to last: Successful habits of visionary companies*. New York: Harper Collins.

De Charms, R. (1968). *Personal causation: The internal affective determinants of behavior*. New York: Academic Press.

Edmonds, R. (1979). Effective schools for the urban poor. *Educational Leadership. 37*(1), 15–24.

Edmonds, R. (1982). Programs of school improvement: An overview. *Educational Leadership, 40*(3), 4–11.

Effective Schools Products, Ltd. (n.d.). *Revolutionary and evolutionary: The effective schools movement*. Okemos, MI. Retrieved July 19, 2006, from www.effective-schools.com/downloads/Revolutionary.pdf

Faltis, C., & Wolfe, P. (Eds.). (1999). *So much to say: Adolescents, bilingualism, and ESL in the secondary school*. New York: Teachers College Press.

Finn, J. D. (2006). *The adult lives of at-risk students: The roles of attainment and engagement in high school* (NCES 2006328). Washington, DC: National Center for Education Statistics.

Fisher, C. W., Berliner, D. C., Filby, N. N., Marliave, R., Cahen, L. S., & Dishaw, M. M. (1981). Teaching behaviors, academic learning time, and student achievement: An overview. *Journal of Classroom Interaction, 17*, 1–15.

Gándara, P., & Bial, D. (2001). *Paving the way to higher education: K–12 intervention programs for underrepresented youth.* Washington, DC: National Postsecondary Education Cooperative.

Goldenberg, C., Gallimore, R., Reese, L., & Garnier, H. (2001). Cause or effect? A longitudinal study of immigrant parents' aspirations and expectations and their children's school performance. *American Educational Research Journal, 38*(3), 547–558.

Goddard, R. D., Hoy, W. K., & Woolfolk Hoy, A. (2004). Collective efficacy: Theoretical developments, empirical evidence, and future directions. *Educational Researcher, 33*(3), 3–13.

Greenleaf, R. K. (2008). *The servant as leader* (rev. ed.). Westfield, IN: Greenleaf Center for Servant Leadership.

Hafner, A., Ingels, S., Schneider, B., & Stevenson, D. (1988). A profile of the American eighth grader: NELS:88. Washington, DC: National Center for Education Statistics.

Hargreaves, A., & Fink, D. (2005). *Sustainable leadership.* San Francisco: Jossey Bass.

Hoy, W. K., Tarter, C. J., & Woolfolk Hoy, A. (2006). Academic optimism of schools. In W. K. Miskel & C. Miskel (Eds.), *Contemporary issues in educational policy and school outcomes* (pp. 135–156). Greenwich, CT: Information Age.

Jordan, W. J., & Plank, S. B. (2000). Talent loss among high achieving poor students. In M. Sanders (Ed.), *Schooling students placed at risk: Research, policy, and practice in the education of poor and minority adolescents.* Mahwah, NJ: Lawrence Erlbaum.

Kahn, C. Arizona above national average for dropout factories. Retrieved November 20, 2009, from http://www.azstarnet.com/sn/hourlyupdate/208922.php

Karweit, N., & Slavin, R. E. (1981). Measurement and modeling choices in studies on time and learning. *American Educational Research Journal, 18*(2), pp. 157–171.

Kindler, A. (2002). *Survey of the states' limited English proficient students and available educational programs and services: 2000–2001, summary report.* Washington, DC: National Clearinghouse for English Language Acquisition and Language Instruction Educational Programs.

Kleiner, B., Porch, R., & Farris, E. (2002). *Public alternative schools and programs for students at risk of education failure: 2000–01.* Washington, DC: National Center for Education Statistics.

Leonard, L. (2008). Preserving the learning environment: Leadership for time. *International Electronic Journal for Leadership in Learning, 12.* Retrieved on February 12, 2010, from http://calgary.ca/lejill/leonard2008.

National Academy of Education. (2009, September). *Standards, assessments, and accountability: Education policy white paper.* Washington, DC: Author.

Natriello, G., Pallas, A. N., & Alexander, K. L. (1989). *Pathways to college network.* Retrieved December 3, 2008, from www.pathwaystocollege.net

Nichols, S. L., & Berliner, D. C. (2007). *Collateral damage: How high-stakes testing corrupts America's schools.* Cambridge, MA: Harvard Education Press.

Norrid-Lacey, B. A. (1998). *Dreams I wanted to be a reality: Experiences of Hispanic immigrant students at an urban high school.* Ph.D. Dissertation, AAT 9837690. Arizona State University.

Pimentel, R. (2002, May 19). Empty chair, empty future in Yuma: A school that's way ahead of the curve (Opinion). *The Arizona Republic,* p. vi.

Plank, S., & Jordan, W. J. (2001). Effects of information, guidance and actions on postsecondary destinations: A study of talent loss. *American Education Research Journal, 38*(4), 947–949.

Roderick, M. (2006,). *Closing the aspirations achievement gap: Implications for school reform. A commentary from Chicago.* Paper, prepared for MDRC's 2005 high school reform conference. Retrieved January 28, 2010, from http://www.mdrc.org/publications/427/overview.html

Rutter, M., Maugham, B., Mortimore, P., & Ouston, J., with Smith, A. (1979). *Fifteen thousand hours: Secondary schools and their effect on children.* London: Open Books.

Sacks, P. (2007). *Tearing down the gates: Confronting the class divide in American education.* Berkeley: University of California Press.

Sergiovanni, T. J. (1992). *Moral leadership: Getting to the heart of school improvement.* San Francisco: Jossey Bass.

Smith, B. N., Montagno, R. V., & Kuzmenko, T. N. (2004). Transformational and servant leadership: Content and contextual comparisons. *Journal of Leadership and Occupational Studies, 3*(4), 80–91.

Swanson, C. B. (June 2009). Gauging graduation, pinpointing progress. *EdWeek, 28*(34), 24, 30–31.

U.S. Census Bureau. (1990). Yuma county general population and housing characteristics, 1990. Retrieved December 21 2008 from http://factfinder.census.gov/QTTable?bm=n&laDP-1

Index

About the Author

Úrsula Casanova is the daughter, sister, mother, mother-in-law, and wife of educators. Her own career as a teacher and school principal in Rochester, New York, was followed by 4 years as a senior researcher at the National Institute of Education in Washington, D.C. She received her Ph.D from Arizona State University in 1985 and joined its faculty in 1987. Since then she has authored or co-authored numerous articles and book chapters, including *Modern Fiction about School Teaching* (with J. Blanchard, 1996); *Putting Research to Work in Your School* (with D. C. Berliner, 1996), *Bilingual Education: Politics, Practice and Research* (with B. Arias, 1993); *Elementary School Secretaries* (1991); and *Schoolchildren at Risk* (with V. Richardson, P. Placier, & K. Guilfoyle, 1989). She is also co-author of a series of Readings in Educational Research for the National Education Association. Her work in translating research to practice won her an award from the American Educational Research Association.